SURVIVING IN-VITRO FERTILIZATION

IVF STORIES AND INSPIRATION

FROM THE WOMEN WHO HAVE BEEN THERE

by Karen Daniels

The obligatory legal stuff

Please do not resell this information as your own but feel free to excerpt portions for the purposes of helping someone on their life journey – author credit appreciated.

ISBN-13: 978-1463678814

ISBN-10: 1463678819

For more information about ivf or ivf stories visit ivfcreation.com or visit the author's official website karendaniels.com.

 Books, Online Content, and Creativity Coaching

Faith is a Sweet Spot

Faith is a soft gentle feeling - a sweet spot upon which to rest your fear. I don't know exactly where faith lies in one's body, but you know it when you have it. Perhaps faith is borne out of the fear itself, or the realization that once you've done all you can do there is nowhere else to go but forward. In the end, what else is faith, but your all?

Karen Daniels

dedicated to the strength that lies within all women

Contents

Introduction

I used to believe that if a woman were meant to have a child – she would. In-vitro fertilization, IVF, was only for those who didn't know when they should give up. And then I found myself to be one of those women. But, rather than go childless, I changed my opinion. What the hell!

Even in the midst of infertility and IVF I didn't consider myself infertile. Just having problems conceiving. It was denial, of course, a way of not putting myself in a slot for fear I'd stay stuck there. Each month I longed for pregnancy, and each month when menses began, I mourned. A deep form of grief, as if each unfertilized egg were the loss of a child. Because for me it was. I cried a lot, often when alone for fear of appearing obsessed, which I was. The longing for a child does not diminish with failure, or even when faced with the impossibility of it due to age or hormone levels. I was already in my 40's when I began my IVF journey.

I think I believed that having a child is a fundamental right of femaleness. I never wanted children, even well into my 30's. I was too selfish, and knew it, and didn't want my life changed in that way. So I went along my merry way and then it started to creep in, the need, the longing. It was as if I'd grown past my wanting to live only for myself. I wanted something more, something bigger, something beyond me. And then I got married and we tried to get pregnant. Months passed. No pregnancy. That marriage ended and with it, for awhile, my desire for children.

I moved on and went into a long period of self examination and eventually reconnected with someone I'd known long before. Again, wanting children came back to haunt me and we tried to conceive for a year before admitting that we had to seek help. I assumed the problem was me because of my age, and since I had not conceived in my previous marriage.

As a woman, it's very difficult to accept that you are infertile. For a long time I felt betrayed by my body and I spent time trying to bring my energy into a place where my body could function normally, so I could conceive 'naturally.' I wondered, if it couldn't work that way, was it not meant to be?

Or had I created the IVF journey in my life in order to learn something from it? I had no answer to this but the deep seated and firmly implanted need for a child drove me forward. I could not accept no children. Oh, I knew I could go on, and do things and even be whole, for I was. But this something more that are called children are the one thing you can't move away from once they're here. So even as I questioned whether it was right, we moved forward with IVF. I finally came to rationalize it like this; if I had a health problem I would seek whatever medical help needed to get well. IVF is a health problem, not a moral problem. I needed help to 'get well.'

As I edit this book, the stories contained here are a look back, for a few years have since passed. And I am a mom. I had my first child when I was 46, and then I had twins at 48. (My whole journey is laid out in my book *In-vitro Fertilization: The Ultimate Reality Game*).

Many things happened along the way. Some horrible. Some great. One of the great things was the women – the amazing, strong, powerful women who were living in the IVF trenches with me, going back for more in their quest to become MOM. These are the IVF veterans. Some of their stories are contained in this book.

IVF is, on your best days, a journey that empowers you toward your ultimate goal of being a mom. And on your worst days it's a nightmarish-depressing-energy-sucking-black-hole from which you feel you'll never emerge.

Yet emerge you will. Every woman always does, in one form or another.

The stories contained in this book are from women who have been there, in the IVF trenches. They all have a story to tell, and some hard-earned thoughts they want to share with other women who are considering, or just starting, the IVF road.

May your IVF journey be short and fruitful.

Karen Daniels

IVF Cycle Overview

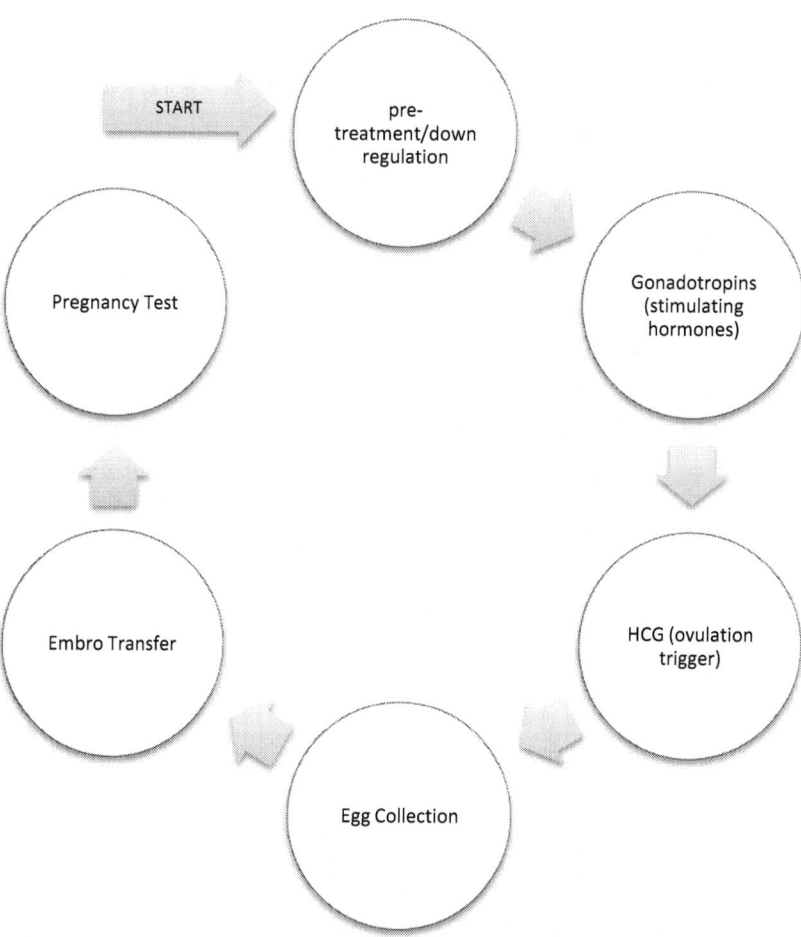

Karen Daniels

A "Typical" IVF Cycle

Of course, the title of this section is a misnomer because there is really no such thing as a typical cycle as each woman's body is different, and every doctor does it differently. This is only a very basic guideline to give you the idea of what happens when.

Day 1: 1st day of heavy menses: AM Dose of injected Lupron. PM Dose of Gonal F and HMG (human menopausal gonadotropin – a mixture of lutenizing hormone and follicle stimulating hormone).

Day 2: AM Dose of injected Lupron. PM Dose of Gonal F and HMG.

Day 3: AM Dose of injected Lupron. PM Dose of Gonal F and HMG.

Day 4: AM Dose of injected Lupron. Ultrasound and estradiol blood test. Result determines dose change.

Day 6: AM Dose of injected Lupron. Ultrasound and estradiol blood test. Result determines dose change.

Day 8: AM Dose of injected Lupron. Ultrasound and estradiol blood test. Result determines dose change.

Day 9: Tentative Ultrasound and estradiol blood test

Day 10: Possible Day of HCG shot. HCG is human chorionic gonadotropin which stimulates ovulation.

Day 11: Start antibiotic in PM.

Day 12: Egg retrieval, sperm needed.

Day 13: Fertilization check

Day 14: Embryos are not disturbed

Day 15: Day 3 embryo transfer if being done (or 2 days from now, 5 day transfer)

Day 26: Progesterone and estradiol blood test

Day 29: Pregnancy Test; Beta HCG, progesterone and estradiol test.

Come Home, a poem

What if my child never comes home
to nestle in my womb
to suckle
to call me Mom?
Where will I go?
What will I do?
Who will I be?
Still me
though less so
sadder
older
still yearning.
What if there is no dancing
no singing
no hope?
Those little feet
to hold in my hand
I think of this
and smile.
I think of this
and cry.
Come home baby, come home
to be with me.

IVF Stories and Advice
by women who have been there

The following stories, thoughts, and advice, were shared with me by IVF veterans; women who have been through in-vitro more than once, in the hopes that they could help others thinking of, or going through, in-vitro fertilization.

Note - all doctor's names have been abbreviated and other identifying facts have been modified. Beyond that, these stories are just as these women lived, and wrote about, them.

Ms. X's Story

From miscarriage, to donor eggs, to twins, this is Ms. X's story.

I went off birth control pills three years ago when I was 29. I wasn't really ready or trying to become pregnant, but felt open to it and wanted to be in a position to get pregnant. Several months before I turned 30 I suddenly felt ready so my husband and I began trying, but without ovulation kits or much thinking. After a few months I realized I needed a little help figuring out the right timing so we began using the ovulation kit.

Six or seven months later, after very diligent trying, I became pregnant. We were thrilled and relieved. Days before finding out I was pregnant, my husband and I met with my OB to discuss why we had not yet conceived. She sent my husband for sperm analysis. Two days after I received my positive we received a call from the OB explaining that my husband's sperm was problematic (6% morphology) and she was very happy we were pregnant because otherwise we would need IVF. At 7 weeks after seeing a heartbeat I miscarried. We were devastated and moved to IVF. Three months after the miscarriage we began IVF #1.

I wasn't a very good responder (few follicles/eggs) but managed to get pregnant. Again, we were very happy and relieved. At 8.5 weeks I miscarried again. Once again I had a d&c and tissue biopsy. Again it was "normal." I had full immune workup and it was determined that I have inherited thrombophilia and was told I would need lovenox when pregnant again. Two months later I did another cycle. It was negative.

I went directly into cycle #3; negative. Before #4 my RE suggested exploratory laparoscopy because he thought I had endometriosis that had affected my egg quality and production. I had the laparoscopy the same day as my fourth egg retrieval. Stage IV endometriosis was determined. Additionally, my tubes were found to be badly scarred. I got a positive from that cycle but knew something was wrong as my beta was low (but doubling) and I was bleeding like a regular period. Ten days later I had another laparoscope's to remove my ectopic pregnancy and cauterize the tube. I was enormously depressed after this experience and decided I was done taking stimulation drugs and wanted to move to donor eggs.

A donor was chosen for me and I liked the description of her. As the cycle approached six weeks later I became apprehensive about giving up on my eggs. I decided to cycle with the donor. I was lucky that our cycles were almost exactly the same. I started stimulation drugs a couple days ahead of her but we both had our egg retrievals on the same day. At embryo transfer day I had five embryos from my eggs that were okay looking and eighteen great looking ones from the donor. We transferred three of mine (5, 6, 8 cell) and four of hers (all 8's or better). Eight days after my three day transfer I learned I was pregnant. A couple weeks later I learned I was carrying twins.

Do family and friends know you've been through/are going through IVF?

Everyone knows about our IVF's and miscarriages. We were very open about our cycles and our diagnosis'. However, no one outside of my parents has any idea we used donor eggs, nor do ever plan to share this information with anyone including our children.

How has infertility affected your life?

I became quite depressed after cycle #3 failed and sank even lower after the ectopic pregnancy. The whole process became enormously overwhelming and I questioned whether I would ever experience a successful pregnancy. Not only was I worried that it could take countless cycles to conceive again, I was very anxious that I would have another miscarriage. That is part of what influenced my decision to go with donor eggs. I felt as though miscarriage was more likely than not and I was anxious about taking more stimulation drugs and further increasing my health risks from them. I was relatively unhappy during this time, but it did not adversely affect my marriage or my work. I really enjoyed work because it was a good distraction and my marriage thrived under this burden. My husband and I became closer and began imagining our life without children. We took a wonderful, romantic trip to Paris after the ectopic pregnancy and I came back prepared to give IVF one last chance and really felt that if it didn't work I/we would be ok. I really snapped out of the funk I had been in all summer and began re-appreciating my life as it was.

Would your life be okay if you didn't have children? How many children would you like to have?

I think my life would be ok without kids if it had to be that way. I used to think I would never adopt, but now am not so sure. I would be very sad to not be able to be a mother and not watch my husband be a father but I no longer think my life would be ruined by being childless.

I think being a parent will be enriching and fulfilling and challenging, and I would be upset to miss the experience. But, my life is already wonderful in many ways that I had lost sight of during IVF and I would concentrate my energies on other areas of my life if being a parent weren't a possibility. All in all, while certainly not my first choice, I don't believe it would be the horrible fate I once thought it was. Before being pregnant with twins, I always wanted one child. My husband and I are both only children and I used to joke that we weren't qualified to have more than one kid. I loved being an only child so to me it seemed like the way to go. However, since the moment I found out I was having twins, two seems ideal. I am a very good adapter. If I had been pregnant with one, I would not go through another IVF again. I would be happy if I 'found' myself pregnant, though.

Name some things you've used to help cope with infertility.

I have certainly done my share of crying and hiding in bed. The real way I coped was to keep on going. Doing my cycles back to back kept me sane. I would have fallen into a much deeper depression if I had had long periods of waiting between cycles. I was not in therapy during any of my IVF's but returned when I found out I was pregnant. I knew I would need support to get me through pregnancy and all of my fears surrounding it.

Taking what you know now, what decisions/things would you do differently at the beginning of your IVF journey if you could start over?

I wouldn't change anything. It took two miscarriages to do immune tests. It took a couple failed cycles to identify the endometriosis. I wish I had had that info going into IVF, but it is unrealistic to think we could have figured it out without the failures to guide us.

Do you think infertility makes/ will make you a different kind of mother than someone who got pregnant in the 'traditional' way? (Whether you've been successful with IVF, adopted, or are still trying)

I think infertility makes motherhood a very conscious decision, whereas for many women without infertility motherhood is more inevitable. To go through the physical and emotional (not to mention economical) toll of IVF you have to be wholly unambivalent about motherhood. I have many friends who say they would not have been willing to endure what I have to become a parent and I can't help but wonder what kind of mothers they are/will become. I feel extremely fortunate and grateful to be given the opportunity to become a mother. It truly is a privilege and I know I will be a better parent having been through so much to get there.

What advice would you give to someone just starting on the IVF journey?

I would say it can be easy for some and grueling for others. I would warn that it is far from a sure thing and to be prepared to do several cycles before succeeding and that for some, success can be elusive. IVF can be a sprint or a marathon.

Author note: Ms. X is now the proud mother of thriving twins.

Bianca's Story

From ectopic pregnancy, to damaged fallopian tubes and repeated IVF cycles, this is Bianca's story.

Karen Daniels

I am almost 38 and my hubby is almost 41. We've been together for 7 years. We thought it was time I stopped taking the pill when I was 34. We assumed it would take a year to get my body back on track; I had been on the pill since I was 19 after a terrible experience with an IUD. We are avid scuba divers and went on holidays to Fiji to dive to our hearts content. I had my period in that time and it was quite heavy and painful and I kept spotting all through the holidays. We live in Adelaide South Australia, but my hubby's parents are in Melbourne and we dropped by on the way back home. There was this feeling in the back of my head something wasn't right. You know that sixth sense that sometimes hits you and tells you all is not well? I decided not to wait till we got back to Adelaide but pop in to the local GP to get some reassurance. After telling the story, the doctor decided to do a pregnancy test just in case. I distinctly remember snickering, yeah, right; it's funny how some moments are clearly etched in your memory.

But it was positive. And suddenly alarm bells went off. He had suspected an ectopic pregnancy based on my story and symptoms and suddenly the possibility rang quite true. I had to go back to my in-laws place and tell my partner that we could be pregnant but that it could be an ectopic pregnancy. We went for an ultrasound and they saw some blob in the right tube. So 2 hours later I was admitted to hospital. Can you imagine? I had been diving with this to 40 meters. Okay, the local specialist did the laparoscopy. He said it would take 20 minutes. Well it took 2.5 hours and I nearly died of blood loss. Turns out that it wasn't in the right tube, it was in the left, but lo and behold, both tubes were irreparably damaged. Remember that IUD I referred to? Well, no idiot would give 19-year-old girls these devices anymore; they cause PID and scarring to the tubes. When I was young, that wasn't known yet. Or nobody cared enough.

So that was the start of it all. Back in Adelaide, we went to the best of the best in Reproductive Medicine. He gave us a choice, which wasn't really a choice: try ourselves and have more ectopics, or clean up the tubes and go for IVF. We had no idea what IVF was really about. Technically yes, we understood the concept but as to the ramifications to our psyche and our lives, we had no idea. We thought about it for a week or two and then decided to go for IVF. My partner received a wakeup call when he thought he nearly lost me. He did not want to go through that again. Let me explain a little bit about us. We are professionals in IT. We are both highly logical, rational people. We manage million dollar projects, people, budgets, the whole nine yards. So we embarked on Project Baby. More about that later.

To me, the diagnosis of infertility had a profound effect. For weeks after the laparoscopy to remove the growing embryo, I was talking to the little "baby" we lost. I admit, we weren't really ready to become parents yet, but in a way we were. We just couldn't keep it. When life turns around on you in one day, you change. I could not believe that this would happen to me. To us. I have been very healthy the last 10 years. Eat well, exercise, the works. The emotion that you hear so much about surfaced in us as well: I would have never ever thought that we could not become parents the "normal" way. For years the focus was on avoiding pregnancy. And suddenly you are faced with the fact that you are labeled. I am infertile. Infertile. What does that mean really? I am a thinker; I think things through all the time and am probably quite good in rationalizing and voicing emotions. But to really feel them is something different. I could not fix this. I could not sit down and write down the problem, go through solutions and pick the best one based on constraints and requirements like I do when I manage a project. Suddenly the way I saw myself changed. I felt less as a woman. Life lost a little bit of its shine. I never quite got it back.

And I felt guilty. Could I have done something to avoid this? Could I have known? Did I do something terrible in a former life to deserve this? I am not very religious but thoughts of a punishing God did occur to me. And I was angry. Oh how anger ruled my thinking. For years I had vague symptoms, phantom pains. Doctors put it down to irritable bowel syndrome or even psychosomatic symptoms. If only I had been taken seriously, maybe this would not have happened. Why me? Junkies get pregnant every day, delivering cocaine and heroin addicted babies. Why us? I could think of nothing else. When both my tubes were removed (they had filled with fluid and the consensus is that that would interfere with the IVF). I felt maimed. Robbed of a piece of myself. It really was a grieving process and it still hits me sometimes, three years later.

We went through the usual battery of tests, HIV, antibodies, sperm to gauge if we would be candidates for IVF. Luckily we did not have a male factor. I truly believe that women can deal with infertility better than men. Although our reproductive organs and ability are intrinsically interwoven with our sense of womanhood, I believe it is harder for men to accept that their "little swimmers" do not work. We saw it as a Project. Talked to nurses and doctors in timelines, statistics, and rational ways of dealing with what was to come. Did research on the Net, read, asked questions. A lot of the time I felt I was not given enough information. Doctors have always had a tendency to not treat patients as peers or adults. Do As I Say, the doctors seem to tell you, Hand Yourself and Your Money Over To Me and I Can Heal You. Maybe. I felt like I had to surrender every bit of control to people who did not tell me what was going to happen. Ah, yes they gave us a video and some brochures but that was not enough. We were two people dealt a hand by life that left them out of control. I wanted to be back in control. So when a nurse or a doctor told me something, I went out and found information. I asked questions, brought articles and research papers to appointments. Wrote things down, challenged, queried.

You know what I found?

Treatment is based on what is convenient for the clinic. They've been doing this for a long time and doctors' opinions are not necessarily what is best for me as an individual. There are so many different opinions on what works, and what doesn't, based on a clinic or doctor's openness to try new things, and listen to their patients as a purchaser of a service. Nurses who told me my hormone levels were fine. Well, quantify and qualify fine to me. Treat me like a professional, like a person, not like a child. I need help with conceiving, not with some lack of intelligence. There is no treatment for that anyway.

Our first IVF cycle was in October. My partner was optimistic, and so was I. Although you try to temper your optimism, I thought it would work the first or second time. I was wrong. We embarked on this time-consuming journey. Beginning with the first day of my period, and then waiting for day 21 to start suppressing. Sniffing medication that makes you feel like you want to jump out of the window. Then injecting yourself with a substance that makes you swell up and your ovaries feel as if they are ready to explode. Although I tried to involve my partner in this whole process, it is so hard to convey the emotions at every step of the way. The depression and headaches in the suppression stage were difficult to deal with. I was so vague in the head I cannot remember whole days. Then there are the irrational fears that you are over suppressed, under suppressed, not feeling anything, feeling too much, and afraid of ovulating and losing all those eggs. One turns into a blubbering fool, or at least I did. Then going for a scan to see how many eggs were maturing. I had heard of women who were able to retrieve 15-20 eggs. Not me. The first cycle I had 10 follicles maturing, and the doctor was able to retrieve 5 eggs. That never quite improved much, so I had to learn to be happy with the disappointing outcomes.

We called for the fertilization results the next day and only 2 eggs had fertilized normally; the rest were fertilized by more than one sperm. I felt like someone had punched me in the stomach. All this for 2? How unfair! The most difficult thing is to deal with all the disappointments at the different stages of the cycle (aside from the Pregnant Women Conspiracy, you know where you see them everywhere while you want to be one so desperately but you can't). I always say that you compartmentalize these stages and you can't seem to see beyond them. Scan, Retrieval, Transfer, Test. Waiting, waiting, waiting. Hoping and investing emotions and not having anything to show for all this. Feeling like a total failure when your body "betrays" you and only makes a limited number of eggs. Feeling like time is running away from you and nearly hitting the panic button. Not being able to believe that you deserve to become a parent. It isn't the medication, or the inconvenience and pain you go through. You can deal with that. It is the unknown, not having a guarantee, having to deal with going through so much to end up with nothing.

How do you cope? One day at a time. It's a very frustrating process. The first time you can't envisage having to go through it 3, 4 or 5 times. But you readjust your expectations. You feel like throwing it all in, then the hormones wear off and you start thinking about the next time. You laugh at yourself, or try to. And you just keep going. And keep going and going. It is tough to get off the merry go round.

The first cycle did not work. I must have gone to the bathroom a million times to do what the experienced IVFer calls the "underwear checking". Rationally, I knew I only had a one in 5 chance of success. But you hope. You cannot control your emotions. My partner can do that more easily and it causes a problem sometimes when I have to explain my emotions to him and lose the feeling in the explanation. If you try to unravel too much, you lose the emotion and you just don't bother. The danger of growing apart is suddenly looming so you must make a conscious effort to share. So you dust yourself off after a failed cycle and look to the next. Life is on hold. You cancel trips, count days, and think about IVF all day long. Life loses a little bit more of its shine. Being able to create life is precious.

Are we doing the right thing by opting for reproductive technology? Should we accept that maybe it is "not to be"? I hate the well meant but insensitive comments people make. Oh just relax. HEY YOU NITWIT I HAVE NO TUBES, COMPRENDE? Or Maybe God did not want you to be parents. SO IF YOU ARE BLEEDING ON THE STREET AFTER AN ACCIDENT I SHOULD JUST LEAVE YOU THERE AS GOD WANTS YOU TO DIE? Or my sister-in-law enquiring why "it takes so long for you two to have bambinos". I NEARLY PUNCHED HER OUT, WHAT AM I A FRIGGING BREEDING MACHINE? The meaningful looks and comments from in-laws (*we're keeping that little bike and the baby clothes; you never know when it will come in handy, hint, hint*). We had not told them what was going on.

One issue was that we needed to deal with this ourselves. And my partner's mother draws everything towards her. She gets upset and suddenly all eyes are on her. This sounds mean and horrible, but she is in the middle of menopause and everything revolves around her. Besides, my partner is the No. 1 Son and nothing is good enough for him. We don't want the Has It Worked Yet comments. We've told some close friends who are great and send me little messages on the mobile when we're in the middle of the madness, and my partner's Auntie knows as she was a nurse in the hospital where I lost our first little blobbie. She has not told anyone and she won't. Some people at work, who I've told, suddenly felt it necessary to tippy toe around me. At two separate instances, people came to see me to tell me "themselves before I heard through the grapevine" that they were pregnant. So what do they expect exactly, that I'd break out in tears and throw myself on the floor in a fit?

Cycle number two started on New Year's Eve. We were camping in Picinninie Ponds with our friends who know about our IVF and I started my suppression that night. The batch of Synarel was OK38, my partner's age at the time and we thought it was a great omen. I was so positive that time, ready to rumble. My dose of gonal-f was increased to 225 to try and recruit more eggs so we could have some to freeze. I had become quite involved in IVF, helped out our clinic with their web site (I design and develop web sites as part of my job) as well as becoming an active member of an on-line support group. I was sure this one was it. On the scan we spotted 12 follicles, 9 of them large enough to retrieve. I was so happy as I was sure we would get a lot of eggs this time. When I woke up from retrieval and heard again only 5 had been retrieved, I lost it. I was so upset at the unfairness of it all. Increase your dosage, blow up like a balloon for what? The next blow came the next day, again abnormal fertilization like last time. This suggested an egg quality issue and it scared the hell out of me. 3 out of 5 were fertilized and they looked good. So we transferred two and froze one. About 4 days after transfer I started having this metallic taste in my mouth, quite profound. Apparently this is one of the classic signs of early pregnancy, and I thought, this is it! Veins on the chest became more pronounced and my sense of smell increased tremendously. All classic signs. Unfortunately, 11 days after transfer my period showed up. I was devastated. Not again, I cannot deal with this again. Why? They looked so good. I did everything right, no coffee, no stress, and no exercise. What happened? That night I told my partner I couldn't deal with this again, couldn't go through it again and again. I will never forget the look on his face. But, we have to, he said. It is the only way. I tried explaining to him how much it takes out of me, no matter how you rationalize and know it is a numbers game, it hits me right where it hurts. What do we do if the next one fails as well? My love said we would get on the bike again and again until we succeed. Hmm, easy for you to say, I thought, but didn't say.

You hold on to anything. There are all kinds of experimental trials going on in the IVF industry. Growth hormone, L-arginine during stimulation, high protein diet, pineapple after transfer. You try anything. I know of people who tried psychics, relax tapes, visualization, meditation all as a straw to hold on to. This is dangerous as well, this whole focus on positive thinking. It could make women believe that they do not deserve a baby if they have done the whole positive thinking bit or praying to God and it still does not happen. Sometime I hate the restriction and judgment of religion. God never gives you more than you can handle. BLOODY NONSENSE, I CAN'T HANDLE THIS. AND MY DH'S (Dear Husband's) AUNTIE COULD NOT HANDLE LOSING TWO OF HER CHILDREN. Arrggghhhh! The stupid, ignorant, shortsighted and judgmental things people say.

We cannot control what I call Factor X. You can create an environment where implantation *may* occur, where fertilization *may* occur, where a pregnancy *may* occur. But Factor X can either throw a spanner in the wheel or suddenly turn what you thought was a sure-fire way to disappointment, to a surprise outcome. When we were just recovering from IVF two, we had dinner at a workmate's place. They had two adorable little boys running around. When the wife said that she was going to the gym as she had taken medication last year that made her gain weight, I just knew she had gone through IVF. You develop a sixth sense. And yes, after a few glasses of wine she blurted it out. Both her boys were from frozen embryo transfers. And she had gone through 6 IVF cycles before she even picked up enough eggs to do a transfer. I was sure the universe threw her on our path to show us that we needed to have patience and persistence. But then again, I could be disillusioned to believe there is an order to things. The first few months, I couldn't keep my big mouth shut. I wanted to talk about it. My partner didn't. He is quite reserved and deals with things by dealing with them, not talking about them. I deal by talking through, thinking through and writing down. There are a few people at work who know this because I need to take a day off here and there and I do not want any hassles and stress. I know of a few ladies at my company who go through IVF as well. We huddle together sometimes and avoid each other at other times. When I was younger, I did not believe in the maternal instinct myth. I believed that I needed to add value to society in a different way than just being a mother. I still believe that I am more than just this one sided view that people have of me: spouse, girl, woman, employee, bitch (oh yeah), and maybe mom. What I did not realize is how deep an effect my diagnosis would have on my self image. I am woman hear me roar, but feeling less of a woman due to removal of my tubes. Little pieces of tissue that affect how I feel about myself and life in general. I find it quite difficult to make small talk. I hear people talk about clothes and their cars and immaterial issues and I think to myself: You have no idea. You have no idea what people go through, what we go through. You have no idea how lucky you are. You have no idea how you take things for granted.

But on the other hand, I've also met some wonderful people. People we have something in common with, a shared experience and pain. When we talk or write we fall over ourselves asking, do you have that as well? Do you feel the same way? Have you had this? And yes, they all have. We laugh at the silly moments we all have, humor is such an important way of coping with IVF. We try to support each other in a safe way. The stigma is still there. People do not talk about IVF. The religious people judge so quickly so you don't want to run the risk of being on the receiving end of Thou Shalt Not........use medical technology and more crap that makes the hair on the back of my neck stand on end. And some people just don't understand. *Why don't you just adopt.* CAUSE YOU CAN'T START ADOPTION PROCEDURES WHILST YOU GO THROUGH IVF! There is also the question of when is enough, enough? When do you stop and how do you do that? When do you accept that you may be one of the 20% that does not succeed? That takes a lot of courage.

We have had 7 failed fresh cycles and 3 FETS over three years. We have had so many tests to figure out if there are immune issues or implantation issues. We limited our stress levels; we tried anything we could think of. Took time off, did not take time off. Did yoga, did meditation, took herbs and vitamins. Nothing helped.

If I hear another Celine Dion Story I'll scream. Success the first time is rare and you are the lucky one if it does work like that. For most it is hard yakka, going through many cycles, eroding your health, your emotional state, your career, and in some cases your relationship. We are lucky. We have our ups and downs and our sex life has suffered. But we have always been pretty close and we have a vision, together. Currently we are at the beginning of another cycle, number 8. I am doubtful this will work at all, and there are days that I think why bother. That cycle may or may not work. If it doesn't, I am not sure we will do another one. If it does, well, we'll see what happens then. I've had some dreams lately of having twins; I can actually picture myself pregnant. I couldn't do that in the first cycles. So maybe I am changing as well. Being kinder to myself, and believing we are deserving of having a baby. And I still drink my wine. The compulsive cutting out of every little thing that gives me joy in life for IVF is so hard.

Our relationship has changed over the years. I have gone through the valley of despair and my hubby has sailed through not understanding why I felt so hopeless. But we struggle through, hoping for that day that the cloud will be lifted. I am slowly allowing myself to think about life without children, I don't think we will adopt. I won't leave anything behind on this world to remind someone I have been here, but I am sure that feeling will have its sharp edges polished off in time. I've learnt a lot about myself, about friendships, about my strength and courage.

If anything, I've learnt a lesson in tenacity and patience. And for an action driven person that has to be worth something. Doesn't it? And we will succeed in the end, won't we? Can you give me an answer? Someone?

Do family and friends know you've been through/are going through IVF?

Two good friends know, some colleagues know but we have not told family.

How has infertility affected your life?

I have changed a lot, lost some of my joy in life and the spark I used to feel. Emotionally I have gone through every emotion humans can feel. My relationships with people have suffered, due to the fact that you isolate yourself. My relationship with my partner suffered due to the fact that he finds it hard to relate to what I am going through and how the fact that I am infertile has changed my belief in myself. My self esteem has taken a nose dive. I feel so useless. I feel that I am not leaving a heritage behind and have only recently discovered how important this is to me. Physically I have changed. I have gained weight due to the hormones and I have a permanent pregnancy mark on my upper lip due to the hormones. I am not fit anymore and constantly stressed. My relationship has suffered a lot. I have been so focused on IVF that I had no room for anything else.

Would your life be okay if you didn't have children? How many children would you like to have?

My life has to be ok if I don't have children and this will require a lot of hard work. The chance is very real that we will not have any children and we are talking about what we might do to replace that hole. But I never see myself getting over the hurt. I would like to have 1 child.

Name some things you've used to help cope with infertility.

Art has helped me cope, talking to my buddies on the internet bulletin board. Writing things down, and milling things over in my head. Reading books about infertility and how other people coped.

Taking what you know now, what decisions/things would you do differently at the beginning of your IVF journey if you could start over? (if any)

Not putting life on hold, not being so optimistic and, being more assertive in what I want from the doctors. I would have found a less stressful job.

Do you think infertility makes/ will make you a different kind of mother than someone who got pregnant in the 'traditional' way?

I believe that this has made me a different person, so yes; I will be a different kind of mother if that is in the future. I will be more thoughtful, enjoy my child more and appreciate what they bring to my life.

If you were going to give advice to someone just starting on the IVF journey, what would it be?

Factor in that you may not succeed. Start planning for that eventuality early in the journey, clarify your motives for wanting to be a parent and be honest with yourself about that. See it as a long-term journey, but don't wait too long if you feel you might have problems conceiving. Time will run away from you. Don't believe everything the doctors tell you; they are just as driven by opinion as any other vendor of services. Find a few friends who have gone through it themselves and talk about your feelings. Realize you are not alone.

Anything else you'd like to add?

Find something you are really good at and focus on that when things go wrong. We feel like such failures when cycles fail that we need to know we are valuable human beings. Art and craft is very therapeutic and can help express those feelings.

Author note: Bianca redirected her energies into a successful award-winning creative business.

Shirley's Story

From a vasectomy to donor eggs and beyond, this is Shirley's story.

My husband had a vasectomy when he was fairly young and when we first started talking about marriage and children we had no idea that it could be reversed or that there were procedures available like PESA or TESE to extract sperm from him. As a result, we thought that doing an IUI with donor sperm would be our only option for having a child. When I was 41, my OB/GYN put me on Clomid and we tried a DIUI. Not surprisingly, it failed.

My OB/GYN then referred us to an RE to talk about IVF. The RE put us through a basic infertility workup that consisted mostly of blood work and an HSG for me. Since the RE told us that a PESA would allow us to use my husband's sperm, we were told that no sperm analysis was required. The HSG showed that I had one blocked tube, but since my FSH was fairly low for my age (6.9) the RE felt that we were good candidates for IVF. We went away thinking that all that really had to be done was getting the sperm and eggs together. Despite a fairly aggressive protocol, I produced only 5 eggs, 4 of which fertilized. All 4 were of good quality and we were really optimistic. The cycle was negative and the RE said that it was just bad luck and recommended we try again. Basically nothing about my protocol was changed and I produced only two eggs. Another RE in the practice who had seen me for a checkup recommended canceling the cycle, but our RE thought maybe more eggs were "hiding" and advised us to proceed. I remember waking up from retrieval and hearing that they got only two eggs and crying. That cycle was a negative, as well, despite the fact that the two embryos that we transferred looked good.

At this point I started researching infertility on the Internet because I wanted to know if there were any other tests or protocols that we could pursue that would either explain our failures or increase our chances of success. At the follow-up appointment, I asked our RE about immune testing, which he basically discounted, and about changing the protocol from one using Pergonal to one using stimulation drugs that contained no LH. He said that the protocol we had followed (8 vials of Pergonal) was the most aggressive possible and he recommended donor eggs. Although I was not opposed to the idea of donor eggs, I wasn't comfortable with his dismissal of additional testing so I made an appointment with another RE. In talking to him we decided to pursue a donor egg cycle after doing some additional testing. Immune testing showed that I had elevated APAs, but everything else was normal.

I was treated by Dr. A and he was very thorough. He insisted on performing another HSG, which showed that I had some sizeable polyps in my uterus that he said would affect implantation. My former RE never sent over the film from my first HSG despite numerous requests, so I'll never know if the polyps were there during the first two cycles or if they grew between the first HSG in October and the second one in March. In April I had a hysteroscopy and Dr. A removed 5 polyps.

While we were waiting for our cycle to begin, I first read about the SCSA test and asked Dr. A about it. He said that we couldn't do it before the cycle because of my husband's vasectomy, but recommended getting an extra vial from the TESE to test just in case the cycle failed. I also planned to do IVIg even though my NK Cell levels were normal just because I had had two previous failures.

Our donor performed wonderfully and we got 40 eggs. 34 were fertilized and we transferred 4 perfect ones on Day 3. We were surprised to learn that of the remaining 28, only 5 made it to Day 5 blastocysts. The cycle was negative and we were devastated, to say the least, since everything had been perfect. Dr. A recommended doing the SCSA and the results showed chromosomal defects in 91% of my husband's sperm. That would definitely explain the negative as well as so few of the embryos making it to Day 5.

We geared up for another donor cycle and decided not to do the IVIg since we thought that the problem was most likely the sperm. For this cycle we used donor eggs and donor sperm, both from proven donors. We again transferred four embryos on Day 3, but this time 7 of the remaining 10 made it to Day 5. We were very optimistic about this and certain that this cycle would work and I was seriously concerned about the possibility of a multiple pregnancy. We had been advised of the risks at each transfer, but after so many failures we insisted on transferring four.

Words like "disappointed" don't even come close to describing how we felt when that cycle ended up negative. We had done absolutely everything to try to have a child. Everything about the cycle was perfect – proven donors, perfect embryos, perfect lining, and flawless transfer. The only word that comes close to describing how we felt is hopeless. With every other failed cycle we had looked ahead to "Plan B." We joke about needing to have a plan, but the reality of having a plan is that you have hope. Hope that changing something, adding something, doing something different will be what you need to succeed. There was nothing left for us to add or change or try.

Without a lot of hope, we got ready to transfer the remaining embryos we had frozen from the previous two donor cycles. In order to make sure that no stone was left unturned, we decided to add the IVIg back into the protocol and to try acupuncture. If nothing else, the acupuncture would be relaxing and I had had a friend who had failed IVF cycles get pregnant naturally after doing acupuncture treatments for several months.

We talked a lot with our RE about which straws of embryos to thaw and how many to transfer since we had straws from two very different cycles and we had never transferred blastocysts. Despite the better chances with blasts, we wanted to be aggressive and Dr. A said he had no problem transferring 4 blasts. On the day of transfer, we thawed four embryos from the most recent cycle where we had used donor eggs and donor sperm. After three hours, only two of these were showing strong signs of growth, so we decided to thaw two more embryos from the earlier cycle when we had used my husband's sperm. Although I wasn't optimistic about those embryos, when we got to the clinic for the transfer, those two had shown the best growth and were fully expanded. We ended up transferring 5 blasts.

It was really hard to be optimistic during the wait so I just wasn't. I cried all the way home and every night. My husband stayed optimistic until the very end of each cycle and said over and over how he "knows this one will work" and told me to stay positive. I didn't want him to see that his enthusiasm had no effect on me and I was dreading disappointing him again with another negative.

Unlike previous cycles where I had rested and basically acted like a pregnant woman, I just went about life like normal this time. The day after the transfer I had a dinner party and drank about half a bottle of wine. The next day I planted a dozen bare root roses. I drank Diet Cokes almost every day. My RE had said he would break the clinic rules and call me with the results of my first beta on Friday at 7 days past the transfer. When I didn't hear from him on Friday night, I cried for hours and had a glass of wine.

The next morning I realized that I had one HPT in the bathroom and unlike most nights, I hadn't had a lot of water during the night or gotten up to pee. I figured there was nothing left to lose, so I peed away. I really didn't believe it when that second line showed up, but there it was! I went in and woke up my husband and it was like a scene from one of those stupid HPT commercials except I was crying and grinning like a fool. I carried that pee stick around all morning asking over and over if he saw that line and making him tell me it really was there. Later that morning Dr. A called and told me that my beta the day before had been 36, but that he had been in surgery until very late and hadn't received the results. The next beta more than doubled and the ultrasound confirmed one strong heartbeat. But I don't think I'll believe it's all real until I hold our baby in my arms.

Did you tell anyone you were going through IVF?
When we started our first IVF cycle, we told some of our friends and I told my sister. After two negatives, we stopped talking to our friends about what we were doing and told those that asked if we were going to try again that we were, but we were taking some time off. Most people seemed to get the hint and not ask any more. When I was in the 2 week wait of our fourth cycle I didn't go to a birthday dinner at my husband's parents' house and they asked if I was pregnant. He told them I wasn't, but that we were trying IVF. They have no idea he had a vasectomy, so they probably think we need IVF because I'm over 40. With each failed cycle it became more and more difficult to tell people the bad news, so we told

absolutely no one about our last cycle until it was confirmed to be successful.

I have no plans to ever tell my parents we did IVF because they wouldn't be supportive and we decided that we would tell no one about using a donor. We'll probably tell our children that we did IVF and perhaps someday we'll tell them about using a donor, but then it will be their decision whether or not to tell other people how they were conceived.

How has infertility affected your life?

I don't know that infertility has really affected my life in any profound ways. I always knew that I married a true partner, but dealing with infertility has made me appreciate how sensitive and caring my husband is. It has been a frustrating experience and I wish we hadn't had to spend the time, money and emotional energy that we have dealing with it. I'm sometimes afraid that we won't be able to give our children certain advantages and experiences or send them to a good college because we've spent so much money having them, but I'm confident things will work out. Besides, what good would the money be to them if they weren't here?

Would your life be okay if you didn't have children? How many children would you like to have?

I married late in life and for many years I filled my life with interesting things to take the place of not having anyone to share my life with. My life was fun and interesting, but nothing completely filled that empty space. I think that's how my life would be without children. I might travel more, have more time to pursue hobbies or personal growth, have a nicer house, but nothing would ever completely compensate for not having children. If I can, I'd like to have two children. We have four more embryos on ice. We've decided that as soon as possible after having this baby, we'll thaw those four and give it another try. If it doesn't work, we'll be happy with one. At our age (early 40s) we want to spend our time enjoying what we have instead of trying to have more (of anything).

Name some things you've used to help cope with infertility.

For my entire life I have dealt with stress and unhappiness by exercising and doing outdoor activities like hiking and mountain biking. Once I started IVF it became more difficult to exercise on a regular basis. After a failed cycle, I'd just get my fitness back and it would be time to start over again. Not being able to relieve stress by exercise made the whole experience much more frustrating. I was lucky enough to find an amazing group of women through an Internet site who became an invaluable source of support and information. I think I probably would have given up if it hadn't been for them.

Taking what you know now, what decisions/things would you do differently at the beginning of your IVF journey if you could start over? (if any)

I'm afraid that what I would have liked to have done differently is impossible. Because infertility isn't discussed openly, it would have been impossible to do the kind of research I do before starting any other kind of project. For example, if you're going to remodel the kitchen you ask all your friends if they've ever done a remodel and if so, can they recommend a good contractor. And if you're at a party with strangers, you have no qualms about asking the same questions. People don't deal with infertility like that, so you can't get the same kind of information and opinions that you would about anything else. And this is so much more important! You just go see the person that your OB recommends and trust that they know what they're doing.

Do you think infertility makes/ will make you a different kind of mother?
I don't know that infertility will make me a different kind of mother than someone who got pregnant the traditional way since I can't imagine that the way you conceive makes you love your children any more or any less. I am certain, however, that having gone through what we've gone through to have a family will mean I'll never take our children for granted.

If you were going to give advice to someone just starting on the IVF journey, what would it be?
My one piece of advice to people starting out on an IVF journey would be to research everything you can before your first appointment and ask a lot of questions. If possible, interview at least two different REs and compare the protocols they suggest. Insist on having every possible test before starting out, even if your RE thinks he or she has the problem identified. We started out thinking all we had was a male factor of vasectomy! Our first RE thought that the vasectomy and one blocked tube were our only issues. By the time it was over, we learned about the polyps, the other male factor, being a poor responder and needing donor eggs, and the immune issues. It was an expensive learning process, a lot of which could have been avoided by about $1500 worth of additional testing.

Anything else you'd like to add?

One additional thing - dealing with infertility and multiple failed IVF cycles is the hardest thing I've ever done. So much of the pain and frustration is endured alone and only another woman who has gone through it truly understands what you're going through. Even the most caring husband can never fully understand. If possible, anyone going through IVF should find a support group. Getting support from other women is truly a blessing, but giving support is what will really make you stronger.

Author note: Shirley is now the proud mother of her young daughter.

Monica's story

From varicocele surgeries to more than two years of IVF, this is Monica's story.

Monica and her husband have been trying to conceive for five years. Her husband has had 2 varicocele surgeries, with each requiring 6 months recovery. As of this interview, Monica has spent exactly 2 years dealing with in-vitro fertilization. This includes 5 fresh cycles and 1 FET.

Do family and friends know you've been through/are going through IVF?

My immediate family (parents, grandparents, sister, brother, in-laws) know every little detail and I've told only 5 friends. The rest have no idea.

How has infertility affected your life?

ME THEN	ME NOW
200K in the bank	Dead broke in a one bedroom rental
Fit, muscular type	Fat and lazy
Pretty fashionable NY chick	Wear sweats
31	36
Many friends. Easygoing.	Bitter and angry at the world
Well read and politically aware and active. Good advice giver.	Me-centric universe
Best friends with my sister	So jealous of my siblings I can't breathe
New MBA from Columbia Business School in high paying consulting job	Unemployed. Career in the shitter.
Sociable and outgoing	Want to be alone with husband
Secret believe in some sort of God	Atheist
Wanted to live forever	Don't care if I get hit by a truck tomorrow
Dynamic	Dull
Good daughter, granddaughter, sister and friend	Isolated
Great with children	Avoid children at all costs
	BUT...
Madly in love with DH	More in love with DH than ever

Would your life be okay if you didn't have children? How many children would you like to have?

It would be decidedly NOT be ok if we didn't have children. I always wanted 3 but obviously now just 1 would do.

Name some things you've used to help cope with infertility

The Internet boards, eating, crying, smoking, and drinking margaritas after negative cycles, exercising madly between cycles. Also my husband found a couples therapist for us who specializes in infertility. Oh – and spending money we don't really have on travel in order to get away from this crappy reality of ours. During the IVF phase of our IF period we've been to Edinburgh, Utah and Sun Valley skiing numerous times, Cannes, Montreal, Amsterdam, the Caribbean a couple times and London. It always helps a little. But certainly not enough.

Taking what you know now, what decisions/things would you do differently at the beginning of your IVF journey if you could start over? (if any)

Had to laugh at the "if any" part. I would have started off at my current clinic instead of wasting three cycles at another clinic. I would have had immune testing done and started with acupuncture from the get go. I would have started posting on the Internet boards years before I finally did and I wouldn't have let my weight get away from me.

Do you think infertility makes/ will make you a different kind of mother than someone who got pregnant in the 'traditional' way?

That's an easy one. A resounding YES. I know that I would have appreciated parenthood more and complained less if this had worked out for me. My husband and I are a thousand times stronger as a couple and I think that that too would have influenced our parenting skills. We would have been way more on the same page than if we had never had to go through this madness together. I am also a much more empathetic/less judgmental person which I imagine would carry over and benefit a child (but wasn't that bad before – didn't need this – I swear!)

If you were going to give advice to someone just starting on the IVF journey, what would it be?
Oy. Where to start? Be proactive. Do as much research as possible. Get a second opinion sooner rather than later. Even if they tell you you're a sure thing don't believe it (our first Reproductive Endocrinologist told us our case was as easy as they come). Don't feel sorry for yourself and "let yourself go" because if things don't work out for you, you'll have that to hate yourself for as well. Remember that you don't have to go to baby showers or anything that you don't feel comfortable with. Just get over the money part. This will break the bank no matter how you slice it. If you get pregnant don't become one of "them". Remember what IF felt like and – you know – do unto others. If your pregnancy is difficult (and has a happy ending, of course) I could care less about your morning sickness and swollen ankles. I am the WRONG PERSON to share this with.

Author note: Monica is now the happy mother of 3 children.

Julie's Story

From Clomid, to countless failed cycles and a father dying of cancer, this is Julie's story.

I knew I'd have trouble getting pregnant because my mom took 7 yrs to have me and I did not use birth control with my ex-husband and didn't get pregnant. (Although, we were only married 8 months and together for a year total and barely touched each other towards last half of the relationship.)

My current husband and I stopped taking the pill 4 months before our wedding. We wanted kids right away and figured the odds of it working before the wedding were small, and the added eyebrow lifts it might cause may just make it work! The first 6 months, we just had sex and didn't time anything. After that, I started to pay attention more and still no baby. More than one year later we went to an OB whose card also said "fertility specialist." Too bad I didn't know anything then. Anyway, she prescribed Clomid, and we raced home knowing that we'd take this magical pill and hope there was only one baby and not twins! Sad, I know. You are supposed to take a month off between cycles of Clomid, so we waited and tried again. Still no luck. Then we did a back to back, thinking it would get things going. Again, no luck. The OB increased our dose, 4 more attempts. Still no second line on the home pregnancy test.

During this time we also got a sperm analysis, a laparoscopy and hydrosalingram; all normal. Increased our dose again, 3 more tries, back to back. No luck. At this point, I had done 10 cycles of Clomid and asked to be referred to a specialist. While waiting for the referral, we did one more try at Clomid along with an intrauterine insemination. Negative. So, then we went to a fertility center to see Dr. H. I was 28 yrs old. Dr. H pumped us up with optimism. We were young, healthy, I had perfect tubes and ovaries. My husband's sperm count was sky high with 75% motility. There was no reason we shouldn't be pregnant, he said. So, we did our first IUI while injecting stimulation drugs. Again, we thought with this kind of supervision, with all the ultrasounds to check my system, and the powerful drugs, it was a one time gig and we'd be pregnant. I did one vial of stimulation drugs and got one follicle. This was followed by the ever present negative pregnancy test. Okay, maybe I just needed more meds, because everything is fine, right?

Two vials of stims, two eggs, another negative. Three vials, three eggs, another negative. Now my husband was losing steam and motivation, and this was getting expensive. We ask Dr. H if we should keep going. Well, my insurance paid for 6 cycles (not the drugs) so he said we should go for it and up the meds. So we tried again with 4 vials a day. This time we got 8 follicles! Now we're cooking. Surely we were going to get pregnant, as we had paid our dues, right? Wrong. Negative again. This one was very devastating. We decided to try one more time, and then move on to IVF if we could find a way to afford it. Did 4 vials of stims again, got 8 eggs again, and of course, another negative. Now I was pissed. I felt like I wasted 1.5 yrs on Clomid and another 9 months on IUI's. There was nothing "wrong" with us and it was ridiculous that we weren't pregnant yet. It was 2.5 yrs since we had started trying, and I was gaining a ton of weight from the meds and had nothing to show for it.

So, I contacted my husband's grandparents and asked if they would loan us $12k for an IVF cycle. I was sure one cycle would work. (Do I ever learn?). They loaned us the money and we proceeded with our first IVF cycle in September that year. In preparation for the cycle, I did lots of internet research, and joined a support board, IVF connections, in July. It really helped me through. Anyway, since we knew I needed lots of drugs, we decided to up the meds to 6 amps a day. This cycle is when we first realized that I may not have the best eggs. We got 22 eggs, 12 were mature, 10 fertilized. Of course I was disappointed because I had envisioned lots of embryos to freeze for siblings, since of course IVF was practically a guarantee of getting pregnant since they do all the work for you, right? Oh well, I'll just go for twins.

So, we take the embryos to blastocyst, and had 1 great blast and 3 good morulas on day 5. The rest were still developing and weren't so hot. I convinced the reproductive endocrinologist to transfer all 4. As a young person with her first cycle, this was no easy feat. Especially since my dear husband turned ghost white at the thought, since he also thought IVF meant guaranteed pregnancy. Anyway, I was determined to get a baby and so after much arm twisting the RE did it. I spent the next two weeks so scared of quads, and hoped it would just be twins. When I got the phone call, I braced myself for a high number. You could have knocked me over with a feather when the nurse said negative. I was in shock. I broke down and just lost it. The next day my husband and I went and got a puppy. I really needed a little being to take care of, and the puppy really helped.

It took a week of heavy smoking and drinking until I decided I had punished my loser, dysfunctional body enough, and we went in for our "what went wrong" meeting. Dr. H said there was nothing he would have done different and that I must have just fallen on the wrong side of the odds since there was no reason he could see that it didn't work. He then mentioned that there was a study from a pharmaceutical company that was starting, and I could join if I wanted to and get a free cycle and free meds. I thought, my god, with this gift, it must be a sign that I'll get pregnant. I started the program right away and was on meds by December. The day before I started stims, I went in to get the meds. I found out you can't have more than three vials a day. Well, I knew that only gets me three follies, so that wasn't going to work. They basically said, hey, it's free don't knock it. We can up the meds to 5 a day if you don't progress in 5 days. So I went home deflated. When I got home, I got a call from my dad that his cancer had returned after his successful surgery that summer for lung cancer, and that it was back worse than before. He didn't want me to come up since he wanted me to finish the cycle. Making his grandchild was more important to him, he said, than me sitting there for nothing. So, I started the stims and talked to him every day.

We were both fighting for life, him for his own and me for my babies. I think he was rooting more for me than for himself. After a few days of stims, I got a call from my aunt that my dad was in the hospital and in bad shape. I went to my RE appt the next morning, got my dose upped to 5 amps since I only had 3 follies (big surprise) and then my husband and I flew to the bay area to see my dad. We spent the weekend with him in the hospital and most of the other family came. It was clear he didn't have long. I had to fly back on Monday for another appointment, or I'd get kicked out of the study. My plan was to fly back and forth as much as I could between appointments. I came home Monday, and my follicle count had gone up a little. I had another check up Wednesday. A little better but not much. Wednesday night, I got the call that my dad had died. I felt terrible that I wasn't there, but I knew also that he wanted me to get pregnant. But it was still very hard. The funeral was the following Saturday. I was supposed to take my trigger shot on Friday and have the egg retrieval on Sunday. As it turned out when I went in on Friday, my follicles still weren't mature enough to trigger, so they just told me to go up and take the trigger shot Saturday night after the funeral. I did so and came home Monday for egg retrieval. They got 5 eggs, terrible quality, 2 fertilized. The combo of the stress of my dad and the low meds just ruined the cycle. Dr. H said to still transfer, even though they weren't great quality, as he'd seen worse become babies, and maybe all this turmoil would still end up in a ++ cycle. He gave me the old, close a door, open a window line. So, we transferred them and I held no hope and was not surprised when the negative came. We decided to take 6 months off and get our bearings. We would do our last IVF ever that July.

I got a little money from my dad's estate, and we were able to use the money to cycle in July. I lost 30 lbs and got myself together. We decided to do a 3 day transfer. I asked my RE about heparin, since I saw women starting to take it on IVF connections and getting ++ results. He told me I didn't need it. I wasn't too old, and there was nothing wrong with me. I was just unexplained and had really only done one cycle prior since the January one didn't count as it was so bad and the meds were wrong. This time, we got 23 eggs, 12 mature, 8 fertilized. I insisted that we would put back anything that looked remotely healthy and that I was tired of doing this. On transfer day, I had 6 embryos that were over 4-cell. We put them all back. This time, I was numb. I didn't have the same optimism. When the period cramps came before beta day, I knew the results before the hpt could tell me.

I went on IVF connections board and talked to some girls that were going to a different fertility institute and listened to them talk about the implantation factor and new meds that they were using. I went to that institutes site and spent hours reading. I called and made an appointment at their facility before I even went in for my beta test. I didn't care as much this time about the negative since, A) I didn't know anything else, and B) I had a plan. At this point my husband was over doing all this fertility stuff. He felt it had ruled our lives for so long. He didn't want to go to the initial appointment so I went with my mom. She was so impressed with Dr. A and their tests that she offered to pay 1/3 of the cost of the 3 cycle program. I went home and talked to my husband. We agreed to get my blood checked to see if I had any auto-immune issues that were causing implantation resistance. If my blood came back normal, we'd hang up our hats for a few years and get back to our lives. If I had a real problem that someone could finally identify as to why I wasn't getting pregnant then we'd try with them if they had a reasonable solution. Well, lucky for me, I had elevated APA's and only needed heparin. So, my husband reluctantly kept up his side of the bargain and we moved forward.

This time, on the new meds, I got 22 eggs, and 11 were mature. Sounds the same, except 11 fertilized and 9 made it to blast on day 5! This was a good sign. We put back three, since that was the most we could talk them into since we were on the right meds this time. I only had to wait 6 days for beta this time, and did an hpt on day 5. Big negative. I was devastated. It had been a long time since I expected a ++, but this time I really did. I invited all my friends over that weekend for a "pity party" and was going to give Captain Morgan and the Marlboro man a run for their money. I was shocked the next day when they told me that my beta was ++. I almost passed out. It was only a 5, but since it was so early, the RE said it had a really good chance of becoming a pregnancy and that he had seen numbers that low become twins. All my friends still came over, but this time it was a celebration. My husband

and I were so happy, but somewhere deep inside I didn't let myself believe since I had seen a lot of low betas not progress in the year I'd been on IVF Connections board. On Monday, we went for beta #2. In three days it had only gone up to 7. I was devastated. I was ready to stop all meds and get on with my pity party. Except, the RE made me keep on the meds until my beta was 0 "just in case". Two days later I was a 4. Then, finally a few days later it was 0. Between you and me, I started drinking and smoking at 4 though. The period cramps told me it was okay. The next cycle was that next January and it was an FET. Out of the 6 embies I had that were blasts on day 5, only one was good enough to freeze on day 6. The rest had deteriorated. That was scary news. I had one frozen at the new clinic and two frozen at the old one from my first and third IVF. I transported the two frosties from the old to new clinic, and we agreed to transfer all three. I was excited as I had never done an FET and it would be just my luck to do 4 fresh cycles when all I really needed was the less traumatic environment of an FET. Turns out one of the frosties from the first clinic wasn't even a real blastocyst. It was just a mass of degenerated cells and totally worthless. Not the news I wanted on transfer day. So, we transferred two and hoped for the best. Sadly I developed an allergy to heparin and the cycle turned out to be a bust. After the previous chemical pregnancy, I thought it would be easier for my body to get pregnant. All it did was make me fatter. I had gained 30 lbs with my November cycle and another 15 with the FET. The RE and I decided it was best to take some time off and get mentally and physically in shape. I needed to get my weight down, give my husband a break, and get mentally back on track. I was beaten and bruised at this point. I exercised my butt off and tried to be as healthy as possible. After 4 months, my weight had not budged. Finally, after 5 months I lost 10 lbs and while it wasn't the result we wanted, we proceeded with the cycle. This time, I did a lot of research. I went to the RE and told him how the cycle was going to go. I'd had enough and this was my "hail mary". I didn't think I could do anymore after this. I told him I wanted a 3 day transfer, since my embryos degenerate after 5 days, they would do better inside me. I told him I wanted to use lovenox since heparin was making me itch. I told him I wanted to put back anything that was viable up to 8 embies. We went back and forth and he reluctantly compromised at 6, although he still thought three was enough. This time on transfer day, the embies didn't look as good. I had one 8-cell excellent, 2 8-cell fair and 2 7-cell fair and 2 6-cell fair. We transferred the 6 best ones and left the other 6-cell to see what happened. It stopped growing the next day. I wasn't too hopeful, but kept on. I had an hpt that was burning a hole in my cabinet, although I promised myself I wouldn't do it until beta day. I decided to do it the day before the first beta, since it would be very early and probably negative either way. Then I couldn't get depressed at the negative since I'd have an excuse and I'd have to wait 4 more days to get the results of both betas and it would be a surprise for once. I took the hpt and about died when a second faint line came up. I told my husband in an online instant message (romantic, eh?). We both freaked out. He came home and he could see the line too. It was very faint, but there. My friend came over with some more tests. Another one came up ++ right away that night. The next day, I took my beta and convinced them to tell me the news since I had the hpt. It was 13!! I spent the next two days over the weekend obsessing over why it was so low, would it grow or poop out like the last one, and were the lines on the hpts getting any darker. That Monday, the next beta was 98 and I was finally pregnant!

Do family and friends know you've been through/are going through IVF?

Yes, our friends and family all know and have been a great support. You'd have thought they finally got pregnant when we got our ++.

How has infertility affected your life?

IF has ruled my life now for over 6 years. Personally it made me feel less of a women and hate my body. I gained a ton of weight and my self-esteem tanked. I was scared that my husband would leave me because I was fat and infertile. Emotionally, it took me on the worst rollercoaster of my life. I tried to have hope and kept getting my dreams squashed. That is very painful. I walked around for years with a hole in my heart that nothing could fill and very few people could understand. Physically, I'm 90 lbs heavier than my wedding day. I'll attribute 30 to being 9 mo pregnant, and 60 to years of IVF. I don't recognize myself in pictures and have lost self esteem. I have held back from work to focus on getting pregnant. In some ways I think my marriage has become stronger. We went through a lot together and fought a huge war. It was hard on us, but I think if we can survive 6 years of IF, we can survive anything.

Would your life be okay if you didn't have children?

No. My life would not be okay without children. That is what drove the obsession to make this work. I refused to let that happen. For me personally, life would not have been okay without biological children. That made the fight tougher as it limited my options. My husband said he could live without children if we had to, but I know how bad he wants kids. I think there would have been a time when his fight was a strong as mine. Unfortunately, time is not an infertile woman's friend and I couldn't wait for him! I would like 3 children in a perfect world.

Name some things you've used to help cope with infertility?
Smoking, eating, drinking, the IVF Connections board, and the sisterhood of the women I cycled with. I tended to abuse and punish my body for letting me down. It was kind of like, okay, you don't work for me, I'm not going to worry about what I put in you then. So there....

Taking what you know now, what decisions/things would you do differently at the beginning of your IVF journey if you could start over?
I would have only done 3 cycles of Clomid before moving to a specialist, and only 3 IUI's since their success rate is so low. I would have fought harder on #3 to try heparin, since that is what I needed. I would have trusted myself more in the beginning to take more control over the process. You can't just sit there and let the Dr's run everything. No one wants you pregnant as much as you do. You have to drive it, demand what you want, research everything, and make decisions for yourself. It's your life, your body and your dream.

Do you think infertility makes/ will make you a different kind of mother than someone who got pregnant in the 'traditional' way? (Whether you've been successful with IVF, adopted, are still trying)
I think I'll appreciate this baby more than a fertile woman in some ways. I worked hard for this baby and want to

enjoy every second. I won't let her go through a day without knowing what a miracle she is and how wanted she was by her dad and me.

If you were going to give advice to someone just starting on the IVF journey, what would it be?
Same as response above as to what I'd change. I'd also make sure they had a support system other than their husband. You need to have other women going through the same thing that can relate and say the things you need to hear. Husbands try but don't get it the same way. Parents and family are the same, especially fertile ones. And fertile friends, forget about it. They will never get it. I couldn't have done this without the support system of women I had. It made all the difference in the world.

Author note: Julie is now the mother of 2, her daughter created with IVF and then a son who was created the old fashioned way.

Karen Daniels

Forum Support

One of the most agreed upon bits of advice from IVF veterans is that it's important to gather support from women who completely understand what you are going through. And like so many things in life, you have to have been there, or be there, to totally get it.

The previous stories, and the following posts with bits of advice from an IVF veteran thread, come from an IVF support board.

It doesn't matter where you find your support, just that you find it with a group that works for you. Even I, being much of a loner by choice, could not have survived my IVF journey as intact as I did without the help, encouragement, and assistance from some amazingly strong, beautiful women.

The One Piece of Advice

Posts from an IVF Forum

The following nuggets of advice are straight from women who are dealing with IVF. Hindsight is always, as they say, 20 20.

These posts are from an IVF forum, taken verbatim (with permission from the posters) - bits and pieces of information women had wished they'd known at the very beginning of their IVF journey.

(author note, though all the women here gave their permission for me to use these posts, I've eliminated names)

This thread began with the question:

What's the one piece of advice that makes you wince handing it out, but wished you would have heard it earlier in this process?

06-30, 05:48 PM
Vets advising Vets - hard-to-take advice
What's the one piece of advice that makes you wince
handing it out but wished you would have heard it earlier
in this process.

Mine is...

Don't work so hard making dear hubby (dh) feel ok about
his masculinity. Should have slapped the RE that looked at
dh's SA and told him he was in the ballpark...dh is so far
out of the ballpark he can't see it!

06-30, 11:48 PM
Mine would be, don't just live for IVF. I feel so bad looking
back on the last two years of IVF and I don't remember
anything but the cycles. It's like the world outside my REs
office stopped. I wish I would have done more, let go
more, had fun more. It's so hard, but so important to just
keep living.

That's my only advice.
Lately I've been feeling helpless to help anyone. I finally
make it to the other side, but I made it without finding the
secret. I wish I had the answers to it all.

07-01, 12:41 AM
Jeez, this is hard.

Advice is an odd thing, it's not about when you give it, and
it's about when you are ready to hear it, I suppose.

Things I wish I had known back then:

- go seek help for your depression!! I wasted two years being horribly depressed; AD's saved my life a year ago. The hurt is still there, but is so much more manageable and isolated. It is not the insidious disease it once was

- DON'T compare yourself to other people. Yes, some lucky people get pregnant on their first IVF, or even their second or third, you might not be one of them, it does not make you useless, stupid, worthless, etc.

- IF has nothing to do with your sexuality - it does not make you less of a woman, or less of a man (wish all the 'normal' people knew this and would stop offering to sleep with me to help me get pregnant)

- your husband does not and probably cannot truly understand your deep seated need, yearning to have a child, this 'thing' that drives you to obsession. To him it is just a part of his life, not his whole life as it is for you

- sometimes you have to hide the tears (so that your husband won't think you have completely lost it) but find someone to share the tears with, online friends, real life friends, someone who understands, because keeping the tears in will kill you

- Supportive partners, parents and friends are worth their weight in gold.

- People who have never experienced IF for themselves cannot truly ever totally understand what you are going through, however most of them love you and feel your pain. Try not to be offended by their 'advice' or platitudes.

- Try, if at all possible, not to let IF blacken your entire life. It is difficult, but don't wish today away.

- IF is hard enough without having to 'do the right thing' all the time. In other words, if it is too difficult to go to those baby showers – DON'T GO!! You don't need to go. Offer to take the mother-to-be out for a special lunch, just the two of you; tell her it's too hard for you to be there with the rest but you would love to spend one on one time with her. Don't go to events that you know are going to hurt you, when you can help it of course. My friends know that if I say I am not going to come to this dinner or that party it's because I know that I am feeling fragile at the moment. Other times are fine, but YOU decide what's good for you.

- spend time doing things that you love, don't forget about those things. For my husband and me it's getting up early on a Saturday and going for breakfast, sitting and chatting and drinking coffees (decaf!)

- DON'T read the pregnant boards – why put yourself through that!

Can't think of more, I know this was supposed to be about one piece of advice, but I got carried away. Mostly the thing I wish I knew then, in the beginning, is that this is going to take a lot longer than I ever expected. I never, in my worst nightmares, thought I would have done 3 IUI's, 3 FET's, 4 Fresh IVF's, one ectopic and one MC and 3 years later still have no baby!

One piece of advice to those who succeed - remember how hard it was for you when you were still trying! The big difference between those who succeed and those who have not yet, is that those who succeed KNOW. They know IVF can work (for them), remember that for those of us who have not yet succeeded - we don't know, we don't share your sense of conviction. We don't know that IVF can work, or will ever work for us. Don't say "it WILL work for you this time", because you don't know and neither do we. Rather say "I really really hope it does work for you this time".

off soap box. (jeez, how verbose am I today!!)

Good luck to everyone on your journey to become mothers, I sincerely hope that every one of you succeed, in whatever way works for you.

07-01,   01:09 AM
The one piece of advice I wish someone had shoved down my throat 5 years ago -

---Don't walk RUNNNNNNN to an RE office and away from the OBGYNs that think a thirty something year old woman is as fertile as a twenty-something year old. "Oh- you look so young- don't worry - just try on your own for a couple of years"! And here I am no longer a thirty something year old. I asked my OBGYN about trying to conceive (trying to conceive -ttc) every year since I was thirty and was told not to worry.

Oh wait- another piece of advice (who can stop at one). I spent the first year or so "coddling" DH so as not to make him feel stressed - and I was the one being pumped with meds! And my DH is a really a wonderful person. It just took him a little longer to appreciate the ins-and-outs of ttc with Drs poking you. He would have rather we do it ourselves. Now DH knows so much more about the stress of the planning, the doing, the waiting, and the negatives.

07-01, 01:14 AM
Now- I hope I don't P**s anyone off with one more piece of advice that I would have given MYSELF if I had known. (No one else needs to take it). I would have saved some of the earlier $ and tried a surrogate since I have a sneaking suspicion that the problem could be an implantation one....

07-01, 01:26 AM
I absolutely agree with this last one and all of the others.

Get as aggressive as you can and fast. Don't wait for 3 and 4 BFNs before you start testing for immune issues, MF, etc. and thinking about DE and surrogates. The tests are way cheaper and less emotionally involved than cycle upon cycle.

All the best to us all.

07-01, 08:44 AM
I like what D said, about not letting infertility be your life; it took me awhile to realize that and I wonder how much I missed? My other advice to not forget about your marriage, that is what comes first. We spent so much time arguing over who was hurting more and who went thru more and who this whole process was worse on we forgot to lean on each other. We reluctantly went to a counselor associated with our RE group and it did wonders. We finally realized that we married each other for the people we are not our abilities or lack of to conceive. The

counselor also helped me realize that it was not just me who was going thru the pain even though I was the one getting all the meds, procedures, etc., but that DH also was experiencing it as well and it was very hard for him because he was used to fixing things and there was nothing he could fix with this. I also learned how to grieve each month, because each month was a loss, so we learned how to do this together and we are now stronger than ever. So I would tell anyone who is having marriage troubles due to IF don't hesitate to get help, because it could be the answers you are looking for. The whole process has helped me set limits for myself and find peace. While I still grieve over the bio child I may never have. I also know there are other ways for me to be a parent.

07-01,   12:58 PM
I totally agree with G!
My OBGYNs told me same thing over and over for several years. They always told me not worry , just give myself more time to get pregnant on my own six years passed ,it never happened.

07-01,   01:38 PM
I'd have to agree w/G. Don't waste your time w/ the OB-GYN. Get aggressive early w/ testing, treatment, etc. We have to be our own advocates - research, talk to people, get 2nd opinions, etc. early. One dr's word is not the gospel! I could have saved so much time and $$. Also, if you can afford it, go to a top rate clinic right off the bat.

I also agree w/ D about not making our IF our life. Did I take my own advice - no! But, I think I was aware of it. Everything from $$ to work to vacations, everything was planned (or not planned) around cycles, etc. Could go on and on w/ this.

I think both of these are really advice for newbies (esp #1). I'll have to think about that advice that S said "makes you wince" giving it to other vets. I'll post again if I think of one. Great question!

07-01, 01:41 PM
Oh my God!
I so totally agree about the OBGYN problem!

Mine told me just keep trying, when to have sex, and kept on giving me pre-natal vitamins! After about 6 years of that cr*p I wised up and went to a new OBGYN who immediately ordered an HSG, found my only tube blocked, then sent me to the RE.

I agree that if you are over 30 and not getting pregnant right away, run away from your non-helpful OBGYN and find a new one! And an RE!!!

07-01, 04:14 PM
A lesson I learned is that you have to rely on yourself to know when it's time to move on to another family building option. I fully expected my doctor to tell me when she thought the odds were no longer in my favor. But she didn't. All she'd say (after 8 IVF's, PGD showing 70% of our embryos abnormal, and 4 miscarriages) was "well, it's hard to tell a young couple who still has good embryos to move on." I kept pushing her on my odds and kept hearing "well it's hard to say." So I finally said (at age 33), "well, if 70% of my embryos are abnormal now and since egg quality deteriorates with age, would it be fair to assume my odds

of success would be more in line with that of a much older woman." And she said yes. I then followed up with "So my odds of success are probably in line with those over age 40?" And she said yes. I then sought another opinion and the doc was candid enough to put my chances of success at 5% or less. I appreciate his honesty.

So what I've learned is you have to trust your own gut and not wait for your doctor to tell you when it's time to move on to another family building option. I'm not sure what my doctor's motivation was; if she really thought I had a chance, didn't like giving bad news, or just wanted to make more money off me. Sad thing is that while there are ethical doctors out there, IF is big business and some doctors are primarily motivated by money.

Another lesson: YOU are the customer, and you're paying a lot for these service, most of you 100% out of pocket. Don't feel like you always have to play the role of the "nice" and "compliant" patient. Speak up as you would with any other service you're paying that much money for. Doctors are not God, and when they or their office staff is treating you poorly, they need to hear that feedback. Believe me; they're not going to turn away 10 - 15k per cycle just because you offered some constructive criticism.

Next lesson - Go to the best RE you possibly can, regardless of convenience, cost or distance. I've seen waaaay too many people have failed cycle after failed cycle, only to move onto a top tier clinic and then achieve success at the first try. Too many people stick with inferior doctors because they're a mile away or because they're nice, or because they got comfortable there. This stuff is too expensive and emotionally draining to waste time. Go straight to the best, even if it means you need to drive 2 hours to get there.

Final lesson - Moving on will not be the end of the world. Earlier in your journey you might think something like DE is "weird" or that you'd never adopt. Many things that once seemed strange and last resort may very well become appealing to you later on. Don't wait until you've given up on treatment to start researching those other avenues. Hopefully you'll never need them, but if you do, you'll be happy you did some homework in advance. For me personally, I had my adoption applications filled out and mailed the day after my final failed cycle. I'd already done the legwork researching agencies and was ready to move forward. And I can say honestly that while adoption wasn't my first choice initially, I don't at all consider it second best. It's a blessing and a miracle, and precisely what gave dh and me our hope back after many years of failed cycle and miscarriages. There is light at the end of the tunnel, I promise you.

07-01, 05:29 PM
Advice I wish I was given...
... in my young years: don't wait too long to have a baby. The egg aging factor, the difficulty to conceive over 30 and mostly over 35.

Not once was I told this by my mother, my grandmother, an aunt, a wiser though younger friend, my teachers at school, at college ... I paid the price of ignorance: all I knew then was that I would get married (whenever that was meant to be), sleep with my husband and wake up pregnant.

Had I known in my twenties what I know now out of need, I would have made better choices in life and not wasted my most fertile years.

I guess I will never know if I could have had children easily and naturally should I have started earlier.

Advice to young women: get informed about your reproductive issues early on in life and don't wait too long to plan for a family, if you can help it, of course (circumstances in life sometimes make this difficult).

ps: I agree with ALL the above!

07-01, 06:03 PM
If you are young and vulnerable, wear a chastity belt!

End of story.

Oh yeah, and AMEN to all of the above

07-01, 06:09 PM
Tough but true advice:

Sometimes it's better to wait a month or two before your next cycle. Your body and emotional/mental state need to be in prime condition. At times you feel like waiting one more month is the end of the world, but it's not, and can make all the difference in the world in how your body responds and you deal with your next cycle.

Don't forget dh is half of an IF couple. Whether your IF is male or female (or both), both partners are affected. I know everyone is different, and some dh's don't seem to be bothered by IF (or at least so their wives think), but I know my dh was very affected by our IF and IVF. He had as tough a time as I did. Just because he didn't express himself the same way I do, didn't mean he wasn't upset and stressed. In fact, I think all the PIO shots bothered him more than me, since he had to give them to me and he hated causing me discomfort. Anyway, while it's fine to expect your dh to coddle you during a cycle and after a bfn, don't forget to coddle him, too.

You have to learn how to forgive yourself. I never felt so evil and mean before in my life, and I never had problems with jealousy before. IF changed all that. Learning to accept your emotions -- good and bad -- and not judge yourself is a challenge, but important.

The toughest advice to follow is not to let IF overtake and ruin your life. We are all more than IF women. We are also wives and friends and sister and aunts. Many of us have jobs and hobbies. It's important to keep your life balanced and not to focus on one aspect of it entirely. Many of us know this advice to be true, but unfortunately knowing it's true doesn't necessarily make it easy to follow -- so you have to work at it.

07-02, 11:54 AM
If I may add one: research, research, research. Learn as much as you possibly can before starting. There is no such thing as knowing too much (as many doctors would like that to be the case).

07-02, 12:47 PM
My advice is similar to S with a twist. I agree completely, do not stick with your RE because he is convenient, close by or for the worst reason of all, because you "like him", or are afraid switching is disloyal or insulting. You are going to the RE to make a baby, not make friends!

While S recommends "top tier" clinics, I recommend finding the clinic that is "right for you". I went to 3 top clinics and was dismissed by each one for them (one did cycle me twice, but cancelled me both times). Try to find women who have a similar problem to yours and find out where they are successful. These boards are invaluable in helping you network and find the clinic that is best for you (it might not be in your backyard, and may not even be in your state). If it were not for these boards (and the many on the web like them) I would have NEVER found a clinic that would work with me, and my dear daughter would not be here today. It is HIGHLY doubtful many (if any) other clinics would actually be letting me do IVF #13.

07-02, 05:23 PM
Great post S!

My advice is similar to all the great ladies here.

Allow yourself to discover what it might mean to get off the wagon. Sometimes we keep going too much because we try to meet other people's expectations i.e. parents, family, dh. What they want might not necessarily be what you can handle; it is ok to get off.

Don't forget that your worth as a woman is not the sum of being able to have children.

Consciously take time out.

T said it very eloquently - do not forget who you are and your relationship. IF can swallow you whole if you let it.

Realize that the emotions are different at the beginning of the journey and set aside your judgments on how far you would go or what other people should do or feel.

Be assertive especially to people who hurt you with ignorant comments.

Find an outlet, either creative or sports or music. Find some things you are really good at and do those things regularly. We feel so much like failures that knowing you are good at something might make you feel better.

Don't beat yourself up if you feel jealous or bitter; you cannot control those emotions and you are not a bad person for feeling them.

Be honest - and expect honesty. About chances, about success rates, about the reality of IVF. Anything else is a bonus.

07-03,   09:58 AM
Wow. This really was an amazing chain of posts. As a veteran of 3 IUIs and 4 IVF I wholeheartedly agree with the excellent advice offered here.

I think it is so important to be your own advocate - don't go with the flow - make sure that you are getting what you want and what you need - from your RE, from friends, family, dh. I think the REs don't put nearly as much time and energy into us as we would hope - so initiating conversations and ideas and asking questions is key.

My saving grace has been keeping busy. I make sure I do at least one fun thing a day - a lunch with a friend, a stop at a bookstore, a manicure - stuff like that. And I make sure I always have a good plan for a night soon. It helps me focus on things other than IF and THE QUEST and it really distracts me and helps time pass in a happy way.

Best of luck to everyone.

07-03, 07:09 PM
Hmmm. I think all of this has been said. But anyway...

- Antidepressants and therapy for sure.
- Get immune testing early on.
- Start adoption research sooner rather than later.
- Don't let your weight get away from you. Between cycles try to get back in control.
- Be selfish. As many have said, skip the baby showers if you feel like it. Just do what you need to do to stay sane.
- Travel between cycles. Definitely. Even if it's a financial stretch.
- Top clinic if you can.
- And the biggie is obviously the "be your own advocate" thing. I don't think anyone could possibly emphasize that enough.

07-03,   09:19 PM
Please nobody take offense at this
I agree with everyone's points. I would especially recommend not being afraid to seek out another RE when one doesn't seem to be aggressive enough. You can waste a lot of time and money.

I have one more piece of advice but I don't want it to be taken the wrong way, so I'll try to word it carefully. These message boards are great, but they can also hinder one's thinking at times. I remember when I did my first cycle. I had some brown spotting and spent a lot of time on boards doing searches, looking for people who had brown spotting and had positive betas. Naturally, I found some. And if I'd looked more I would have found people with no spotting and positive betas, people with red spotting and positive betas, people with full flow, no flow, green flow, polka-dotted flow, etc. Because the truth is that everyone is different; every cycle is different; every pregnancy (and lack of) is different. So while you can take certain comfort in knowing that others have similar situations and experiences and have wound up pregnant, it can just lead to more turmoil. So when I read posts like "I just transferred one 8-celled and two six-celled, did anybody succeed with this?" I want to tell them not to bother. You can transfer three picture-perfect 8-celled embryos and not succeed while person B has mediocre embryos with fewer cells and winds up with twins. Be careful how you use the boards. Get as much support as you want but don't really expect them to act as crystal balls to tell you if a cycle will work. You just don't know until beta day, and believe me, the people on message boards are supportive and will no doubt tell you that their cousin had exactly the same situation and had a kid.

The other advice I'd give is not to bond with embryos. I don't call them embies; I try not to think of them as little tiny babies. I try to treat them as something with potential. That way the disappointment of a failed cycle isn't worsened. Until I get a positive beta, I try not to imbue them with actual baby qualities. I feel bad enough with each negative beta; the failure itself makes me cry plenty without imagining each embryo as a little child that wasn't meant to be.

I know this post makes me sound like a real hardass. I'm not; it's just that after many failed IUI's and IVF cycles, I know it's hard enough without looking for extra ways to feel terrible.

07-04,   09:21 AM
Hummm: My Advice:

1) THERAPY IS A BEAUTIFUL THING. Get some, it only helps.

2) STD's are REAL and SERIOUS.

3) Don't compare your insides with someone else's outside.

4) Be good to your infertile friends...we are all in this together.

07-04, 10:56 AM

I'm printing this one out for anyone that is just starting...they can read the advice and decide what makes sense for them at the time but the universal advice here is...take control.

Also note to C...I don't think any of your advice (on this post or others) makes you any harder than most of us. I agree that if you look for something to make you feel better (or make you feel bad) you can find it on this board or others.

As for the embie advice...it reminds me of a post on the old veterans board (not the "old veterans" but the "old" veterans board) with someone upset if her first IVF worked and what she would do with the embies...veterans started counting the number of embies they had transferred over the years...yikes. I think I'm up over 50 that haven't resulted in a positive. I do use the term embie just because it's easier to say and type but I completely get your point.

As for the worth of you ladies...time and time again you show me you are brilliant, compassionate, humourful women that roll with more punches that one could ever imagine.

Next time one of you thinks you are all about ttc'ing... check out some of your posts on yours and other threads... your substance shines through.

Thanks ladies

07-04, 12:16 PM
(God, I love this thread.)

07-05, 01:23 PM

People are different I suppose...when I ask a question, I want the cold hard truth, for example if I ask "my beta came back at 7 10dp5dt, could this be a viable pregnant?" I want the truth "yes it could be, however chances are more likely it is a chemical pregnant, wait for your second beta". I've been in this game for too long for sugar coating.

However, I know some people only want to hear good luck stories. And because I can't lie, I mostly just keep quiet.

07-07, 01:00 AM
Honesty rules
Great thread as always!

T- Like you, I would rather hear the honest truth when asking direct questions like the example you gave. It may be hard to swallow at first, but once you get past the emotional stuff- you really appreciate it because you need to be realistic about stuff after going through so many procedures. It can help in planning your next steps.

07-07, 01:19 PM
pregnant mentioned
Is the perspective of a vet so different? It took me 4 cycles and a miscarriage to realize that nothing means anything until the beta. It still took me two more cycles to finally get pregnant.

Even during pregnancy, you have to prepare yourself for the fact that your 'symptoms' or lack of them are meaningless. IVF and pregnancy are nothing but a long waiting game. Your life gets strung out, as you go from u/s to u/s, appointment to appointment.

Time goes unbelievably slow during both...so you might as well just go with the flow.

On my last appointment, my peri said to me "37 weeks...the time just flew." I let him know that the four years prior to the 37 weeks more than made up for it. Fortunately, he has a good sense of humor, and was able to laugh at the sarcasm.

Ladies...I want you all to know that I'm hopeful that each and every one of you long term vets find success in one way or another. Which road you take to create your family may remain unknown at this point, but I am rooting for everyone to find success.

07-08, 09:27 AM
Wish I could have read a thread like this 2 years ago...
I agree with all.

I guess I've always been the kind of "half empty glass", very pessimistic, quality control by nature always seeing how things can go wrong and what to do to avoid it. Some may not agree with me, but this has been a reality for me. So I'm going to add:

1. Try not to be so optimistic, keep yourself grounded to statistics.

When I did my first IVF, something happened to me, I was so happy....... Hope, faith, a miracle!! , whatever it was I was so optimistic, I thought I was another person. Having faith and being optimistic is such a good thing... But your butts hurt so much and not from shots but from when you fall from that high cloud in the sky. Hitting ground in one split second after listening to these words: "Sorry, it was negative..."

If I would have been a little less optimistic:
....My butt wouldn't hurt as much, from falling three times...
....I wouldn't have gained 30!!! yes, 30 pounds so far...
....I wouldn't have forgotten how to smile...

I guess when we do IVF no matter how pessimistic one can be; we always think we're going to be one of the "lucky ones". It is not until we've tried several IVFs that we finally realize and admit, IVF is like playing Lotto. There are few winners, have you have to play a LOT to win.

07-08, 03:14 PM
Great Thread
Since I don't have a typical veteran history, my advice would be a little different.

First of all - try to remember everyone has a story. Everyone. Although I often think that I have it "rough", I remind myself that others deal with "****" also. And vice versa.

Life isn't fair. Bottom line. And that also works both ways. It isn't fair that my triplets died and so many other women take home their babies. Yet it also isn't fair that I am blessed to be a great IVF candidate- and therefore feel guilty. But it's just the way it is. The sooner that I accept that and take control of the things I can and not feel guilt or remorse over the things I cannot control, the better life I will have.

And as so many others have said- there is so much more to life than infertility. There is so much more to life than even parenting. As much joy and happiness as my living child brings me, she doesn't define me as person. I had a life before- and I liked that life! She has enhanced it but not "made" it. Only you can do that.

And the one most important thing I would tell a "newbie" - IF treatment is not about getting pregnant. Although we all know that- we don't act that way. It's about achieving parenthood. Pregnancy is just a VERY SMALL step along the way. I think so many IF patients are so focused on getting and being pregnant that we forget the real goal.

The last thing (and this would only apply to a newbie) - if you can "only " do one IVF cycle, for whatever reason, don't do it. There is nothing I hate more than to read a post from someone sounding desperate. "I can only do one cycle it just HAS to work this one time". I was truly the "one cycle wonder" never did an IUI, just one IVF - pregnant with triplets YET even going into it, had I done my homework. I knew statistically my chances were the same for the first 4 cycles and I was willing to do that many before saying that IVF wouldn't work for us. If you can't go into it willing to give it your best shot, I think you need to evaluate why you are doing it. Most of us have spent WAY more money than anyone should have to, to try to achieve our dream. Although I can understand financial hardship, I understand even more "where there is a will, there's a way". I know I'm preaching to the choir here! DH and I have scraped and struggled to finance all this and still we haven't had to break down to our last resort yet.

Great thread!

07-08, 03:49 PM
Great thread! C, your advice especially struck a chord with me. Thanks for posting.

I too wish that as a newbie I had someone tell me all this. Having said that, I also believe that I had to walk this difficult path in order to come to some of the conclusions shared here. I don't know if I could have accepted much of it early on in my journey.

Posted by: karendaniels
07-08, 06:33 PM
good thread, S!
My advice would be decide up front what is the most important thing to you in all this: biolink to child, being pregnant, having a child no matter what, being a parent, etc. Then make your decisions based on that and go with what will give you the best odds. I wished I'd listened to my RE when he gently suggested that DE were my best chance--I was 44 (and very high fsh) at the time. Duh. I could have saved myself lots of pain and money and in the end it was donor eggs that worked for me.

Realize that IVF is a process, never say never, or condemn someone else for their decision.

Quick Tips and Advice from IVF Veterans

1. Don't work so hard making your husband feel ok about his masculinity.

2. Don't just live for IVF. Just keep living.

3. If you're depressed, don't wait to get help!

4. Don't compare yourself to others. Some people get pregnant on their first IVF, or even their second or third - you may or may not be one of them.

5. Infertility has nothing to do with your sexuality - it does not make you less of a woman, or less of a man.

6. Your husband probably cannot truly understand your deep yearning to have a child, this 'thing' that drives you to obsession. To him it is just a part of his life, not his whole life as it is for you

7. Find someone to share the tears with.

8. Supportive people are worth their weight in gold.

9. People who have not experienced IF for themselves cannot truly understand what you are going through. Don't expect them to.

10. Try, if at all possible, not to let infertility blacken your entire life. It is difficult, but don't wish today away.

11. You don't have to do the right thing all the time – like go to baby showers.

12. Spend time doing things you love.

13. IVF might take you a lot longer than expected.

14. Don't walk — RUN - to an RE and away from the OBGYNs that think a thirty something year old woman is as fertile as a twenty-something year old.

15. Get as aggressive as you can and fast. Test for immune issues, MF, etc. Tests are way cheaper and less emotionally involved than cycle upon cycle.

16. If you are having marriage troubles due to infertility don't hesitate to get help.

17. Be your own advocate; do your own research; talk to people; get 2nd opinions early. Money permitting, go to a top rate clinic right off the bat.

18. Trust your own gut. Don't wait for your doctor to tell you when it's time to move on to another family building option.

19. You are the customer, and you're paying a lot for these services so speak up as you would with any other service you're paying that much money for.

20. Go to the best RE you possibly can, regardless of convenience, cost or distance.

21. If you have to move on it's not the end of the world. Explore all your options early (such as adoption) so you're prepared just in case.

22. Sometimes it's better to wait a month or two before your next cycle so you can be in prime condition.

23. Just because your partner does not express himself in the same way as you does not mean he is not upset and stressed.

24. Learn to accept your emotions, all of them, and do not judge yourself. This can be a challenge but it's very important.

25. Don't let IVF overtake and ruin your life. You are more than your infertility. Don't forget that.

26. Research, research, research and learn as much as you can before starting.

27. Look for an RE that will get the job done whether you can become friends with him or not.

28. Find the clinic that is "right for you".

29. Consciously take time out.

30. Find an outlet – something you are good at that makes you feel good.

31. Be honest - expect honesty - about chances, about success rates, about the reality of IVF.

32. Don't go with the flow - make sure that you are getting what you want and what you need - from your RE and everyone around you.

33. Seek out a new RE if your current one is not aggressive enough.

34. Message boards are great but remember no one can tell you what's going to happen. Use the boards for support, not as a crystal ball.

35. THERAPY IS A BEAUTIFUL THING. Get some, it only helps.

36. We are all in this together.

37. The truth may hurt but it can help you in planning your next steps.

38. You had a life before children – remember that. Children may enhance your life but only you can "make" your life.

39. IVF is not about getting pregnant – it's about achieving parenthood. Pregnancy is only a small step so keep your eye on the real goal.

40. Decide as best you can what is the most important thing to you in all this - then make your decisions based on that and go with what will give you the best odds.

42. I could have saved myself lots of pain and money if I'd realized being a mom was what I wanted, not having a bio link to my children.

43. Never condemn a fellow IVFer for their decisions.

44. Your worth as a woman is not the sum of being able to have children.

Karen Daniels

Conclusion

IVF can be an emotional minefield. For instance, prior to my first IVF cycle, with no knowledge of the arduous journey that lay before me, I wrote the following questioning words:

What if IVF actually works? I'm suddenly afraid that this cycle of IVF is going to work and I'll be pregnant. Yikes! I'm been dreaming of that for so long I almost don't know what to do with success. Sit back and enjoy pregnancy? Isn't it strange that the adage "Be careful what you wish for" really does mean something important. With each wish fulfillment there is change in one's life. Even if it's a scenario or thing that one truly deeply wants, longs for, and works for, there's a part of the having that's scary. For instance, what do we wish for then? What's next? If your longing for a particular dream fulfillment has been a major purpose of your life there can be a sense of loss when the striving for is done. Moments from now I'll take my first lupron shot. My hormones will be altered. From here it goes on, then I'm pregnant, then I have children, then I'm a mom—but it didn't start with this shot. It started long long ago in a place and time I don't know. We fear change, yet thank God for change because without it we are stagnant; there is no growth. And isn't growth what life is all about? So, I fear this big coming change, yet I must have it. For within the change is a transformation I seek.

I know that, as with anything, it's the journey, not the goal that's important – though we frequently forget that in life. Wanting children opened many aspects of self that I had not previously been aware of. Some of those aspects I liked, some not so much. But all would have remained unseen without this IVF journey cracking me open.

And that is something I witnessed, in every single woman who shared this journey. In-vitro does indeed, crack you open in ways you can never imagine – particularly if you become a veteran; a woman who must muster the courage and fortitude to bare her soul, and her vagina, to stay the course and get where she needs to go – even when she doesn't know exactly where that course will lead her.

I knew that with IVF, and if and when children came, my life would never be the same. Of course, that's easy to say when viewing something as obviously life altering as adding children to the mix of living. But in truth, each and every day we live our lives means we will never be the same. But usually that truth is hidden because most days appear so similar to other days that it's easy to live, eat, sleep, and wake up again without remembering that because of yesterday we are now a different person than we were the day before. Each moment, every decision, alters the course of our life. Yet when we choose scrambled eggs instead of hard-boiled, how can we really see this?

Sometimes the biggest things, the greatest challenges, such as IVF, come our way in life, in order to remind us of what truly matters. So no matter where your life leads you, no matter where your IVF journey takes you, keep that which is most important intact – yourself.

Baby Found, a poem

I hear him-her in my heart
and travel forever and back
to find him.
Under each rock, beside each river,
I look
but he is never there.
Every day I seek, becoming weeks,
then months.
I can not stop knowing he is out there, alone.

Then one day
during my search
I meet another woman,
and tell her I can't find my baby.
Unspoken, she offers me a gift
from her deepest self—
I open my hands and take this treasure,
then pull it close and it becomes part of me
forever.
I know where to look now.
I move to thank her
but she is gone.
I turn around and smile, peeking around the tree,
and there he is,
my baby,
ready to come home.

Talk like an IVF Pro
Definitions and Words to Know

Blastocyst
The goal you'll have for your embryos because success
rates are higher. For healthy embryos the blastocyst stage
usually happens at around 5 days post fertilization.

Cooter Cam
That penis shaped ultrasound device which is inserted into
the vagina to view the uterus and monitor egg
development. For a time, your life will revolve around this
"penis" and not that other one (much to the dismay of
your male partner, if you have one).

D&C
Medical procedure used to diagnose and treat certain
gynecological issues such as heavy menstrual bleeding,
polyps and uterine fibroids; can be used to remove
pregnancy tissue after a miscarriage.

Dreaded 2-Week Wait
That period of time where your life is suspended, you're
afraid to breathe, and you'll suddenly become
superstitious. The 2-week period between embryos being
put into you, and the time when you can have a blood test
to check for pregnancy.

Embies, Embryos
Your babies. At least that's how you'll come to think of
them. After sperm and egg are united and start to split
they grow for several days – those are embryos.

FET – Frozen Embryo Transfer
Miracles. When embryos that have been frozen are transferred into your uterus.

ICSI
Stands for Intracytoplasmic Sperm Injection. What? Basically a microscopic procedure to assist fertilization of the egg by directly injecting the sperm into the egg cytoplasm.

lovenox – blood thinner (like heparin), injected

morphology – for ivf relating to sperm. The measure of the percent of sperm that have a normal shape.

stimulation drugs-ovarian stimulation medications which are used to help the ovaries produce enough follicles and eggs

Totsicles - Frokids – Frozen Embryos
Your frozen babies. Embryos that are frozen prior to implantation in you but to you they'll already be your babies.

3-Day Transfer
When embryos are transferred into you 3 days after they are fertilized.

5-Day Transfer
When embryos are transferred into you 5 days (blastocyst stage) after they are fertilized.

I don't know what kind of future life I believe in,
but I believe that all that we go through here must
have some value.

- Anna Eleanor Roosevelt (1884-1962)

Other IVF Books by Karen Daniels

In-Vitro Fertilization:
the Ultimate Reality Game
a true IVF story

What is it really like to go through IVF? If you, or someone you love, is faced with in-vitro fertilization this true story is a must read. If you want a baby and haven't been able to conceive in the usual way, it can be one of the saddest things in your life. This book will give you hope. Many want-to-be parents who experience infertility and are unable to conceive turn to IVF to help them have a family. The most important thing to know is that you are not alone. No matter how bad it gets, no matter how many emotionally induced roller coasters you must ride until you become a mom or dad, be proud of who you are – even when you are at your worst. This is not a story for the faint of heart. This is the author's journal – verbatim – raw - uncensored. The only things changed are, as they say, names, to protect the innocent. Prepare yourself for the blow by blow ordeal of one IVF veteran who lived, survived, and overcame the ultimate reality game, in her quest to become a mom.

http://www.amazon.com/-Vitro-Fertilization-Ultimate-Reality-uncensored/dp/1456419412

Excerpt from

In-vitro Fertilization: The Ultimate Reality Game

May 17, 2001

At last we've begun. Really begun. I started taking the pill yesterday on day 3 of my cycle. On June 1, I start Lupron injections and then it spirals up from there. More drugs and shots than I originally knew. I already know I'll feel like a pin cushion. My best friend is excited about the kid thing now. We keep talking about triplets and I imagine how that would be—the challenge, the difficulty, the joy of those varied personalities all developing.

As it turns out this agonizing pause of some weeks has been good for my soul. There is a calm in my center where before was the desperate yearning for babies now now now. I am anxious of course but I'm enjoying this phase. It's as if someone came to me and said you'll be pregnant in some weeks. Prepare. So that's what I've been doing. All those things in the house I never did after we moved that were on my list. I painted the master bathroom (it looks fabulous I must say—like an Italian Fresco—warm and alive yet easy to look at). We got some new hand me down furniture. Cleaned the garage. And of course have contingency plans for one, two, and three babies. I've spoken to my mom about her helping. I have a list of women who will be here to assist particularly if I have multiples. I've even researched what happens when you have multiples—the potential for long term bed rest. With that in mind I'm doing things now BECAUSE I CAN. I think this helps keep me hopeful. I don't hesitate to jump in and do and enjoy the very act of doing. This is how we should all live life, full enjoyment of each phase for the next one will be different. This one is so big, from no kids to kids, that you can't miss it but shouldn't each phase, day, of life be perceived as such? For the truth is everything ends. Each thing will come and go and we should enjoy it for what it is. Right now, my last days without pregnancy, without children. It's a time of wonder and a time I am now at ease with, inside myself.

Today we went for another scan to check my ovaries—toknow what's there before we begin. This is the first of many scans. And the schedule. So complex. Drugs for 5 days, 9 days, 17 days, over-lapping days, that I made a calendar on my computer—put a stork next to June and clip art baby pictures—one screaming, one sleeping, one sitting quietly with a stuffed bear—that covers the possibilities. Doesn't it? And it's an attempt to make it fun, to make myself smile when I look on the fridge to see how many times I'll be poked by needles that day. For July, I put pregnancy at the top and a couple possible dates for pregnancy confirmation. Though the egg retrieval and embryo transfer are scheduled for June 22 and June 25 or 27 respectively, I didn't want the calendar to stop in June. Superstitious I guess. Making the statement that it goes on after the embryo transfer. In fact, that's only the beginning. And perhaps we'll keep a calendar throughout the entire pregnancy, sort of quick glance journal.

Starting the cycle makes me feel more proactive. However for now, I'll enjoy our childless state as I know it's coming to an end. Now there is time. Time for long hot baths, time for walks, time for self.

Anger and Depression.
June 7, 2001
There's a black cloud in my head filling me with anger and depression. This is the 7th day of Lupron 10u and the last

day of the pill. I was actually feeling okay up until 3 days ago when the bad mood suddenly hit. This feels so unlike me and I've completely lost perspective on the connection between these shots and babies. Though the shots themselves are not particularly painful there is something about having your soft underbelly violated that's psychologically difficult. Its soft delicate skin is meant for caressing not puncturing.

The day we started the Lupron, the doctor found a rather large cyst so now I have to go back in tomorrow to see if I'm going to have to have it aspirated on Monday. That depressed me. On the up side, the mock transfer went much smoother this time.

It's my anger that bothers me most. Everything is irritating and it's all I can do not to tear my husband a new you know what. He's kind, giving me the shots, but everything he does feels wrong right now. For that matter, I feel that way about everyone right now. This is definitely foreign to how I normally feel. Is my anger coming from fear of failure? Fear of success? Both? I feel as if I'm mourning the old me, the me I've always been. And even though I so much want these children, that little girl in me who doesn't want the responsibility, the little girl who didn't even like dolls, is throwing tantrums. I'm trying to let her feel how she feels even as it fills me with a mass of conflicting emotions. I wonder how other women feel when they go through these phases. I feel cut off, alone. I have supportive friends who listen and help but it's still my body going through all this. I feel this IVF is going to be successful and in that sense this is only the beginning. Maybe that's why it's so hard. Things will never be the same. And I want that. Yet I don't. Is this how it feels to be a wishy washy woman? Kids are the one thing you can never walk away from and I've often walked away from careers, men, homes. It's part of why I must do this. And part of why it's so hard.

Today I saw the cutest 6 month old at the post office. He was smiling and charming everyone. It's amazing how they can captivate an entire room. The mother was young, slim, and healthy. I envied her youth and found myself automatically assuming she had no problem getting pregnant. I waited years so there are more blips in the road.

I watched a squirrel this morning eating a green nectarine from our tree.

I hate feeling this way. I hate myself right now. And the world.

Argh, Hormone Hell.

June 11, 2001
I've become hormonally challenged. This morning my husband woke me at 5 so we could begin the next phase—stimulation drugs. No as fun as it sounds. What it means is now 5 shots a day, as we've added heparin 2x per day to thin blood and help prevent clots and Follistin and Pergonal which is an intramuscular shot (in the butt). Lupron continues at half the previous dose.

The news on Friday was good. The cyst was gone and my blood tests came back with an estradiol level of 18 which gave us the go ahead to begin this morning. So, the news is all good but I feel so not like myself. I can feel an immediate change with the shots this morning. Now my head feels hot inside as if there is pressure and my energy feels, well, rounder. It does seem as if this is a more proactive phase. The stuff before was to shut my system down, a rest before the sprint if you will. Now we're beginning the sprint. I had a weird thought that perhaps humans are striving for the time when they can tell their ovaries to ripen/produce the desired number of eggs instead of just one. Maybe IVF is a way to show the body how to reprogram itself. Reaching for science fiction to make myself feel better, perhaps?

My next appt. is Fri. A blood test, again for estradiol, and then a scan to see how I'm responding to the stimulation.

Last Friday I met with the IVF coordinator. She was full of tidbits and after I told her my husband and I wanted to bring the sperm in with us the morning of egg retrieval she shared some funny stories with me—as in don't put the specimen on the heater or air conditioning in the car. We talked more about the things that I can't do. Starting now. No more wine. Sigh. No caffeine, not a problem, I drink decaf. No chocolate. Also not a problem for me. No baths. I'm not sure if that starts now or after the embryo transfer. That's a real tough one for me. I live for my baths. Even belonged to a bath of the month club. No lifting anything over 10 lbs. Also tough as I'm always doing the heavy house stuff. No intercourse. Until after the first trimester. Yikes! The thing they tell me to avoid here is penetration. Back to being a teen and "the everything but" routine...

It seems a little harder to breathe today. Due to shot? The stress of thinking about the shot? I'm definitely stressed. A skin rash on my arm, a zit on my butt. My body's talking and it's none too thrilled about some of this. At least I have a supportive system. My dreams are wild, nightmarish things. This morning I was crying when I woke.

This is a wild ride, one I wasn't prepared for. The intellectualthoughts have no relationship to the real deal. I'm glad I work for myself and don't have to go 'out in

Karen Daniels

public right now. My mind feels as if it's under water. 11 days to egg retrieval. But who's counting?

June 13, 2001
I've recruited family and friends to do a meditation/prayer on June 21st at 6pm for 10 minutes-geared toward, of course, successful outcome - meaning healthy pregnancy leading to healthy baby/s. This is the first time my family has ever done anything like this so that's pretty cool.

I'm trying to bring myself around to a better attitude and stop feeling like my body is being assaulted. An image from the Gandhi movie popped into my mind— the moment when the men are being clubbed and it "goes on and on into the night." That's what my body feels like. I know that's silly in the sense that this is a good thing. I want this, or at least the end result of this. We don't create any experience we're not in agreement to so on certain levels this is the way I want to get pregnant. Hmm.

My husband is trying his best but when it hurts he gets the blame.

My head is clouded and I know I'm not thinking clearly. I went out to run a few errands today and wondered if I was sharp enough to be driving. Slow reactions, my mind wanders and it's hard to make decisions.

I thought I would be joyful doing this, knowing what I'm doing it for. How much of this emotional response is due to the hormones being injected? I know no one likes to be injected; still, it's not as if I have a terminal disease or something. THIS IS A GOOD THING!

June 14, 2001
A quote I saw yesterday, "Only parts suffer, not the whole."

I am doing much better. Amazing what deciding to have a better attitude can do. With each shot now I think, "one shot closer to being pregnant." I am starting to feel my ovaries, kind of a full, pressurized feeling. Tomorrow we go in for the scan. We means, my friend C is driving me down. She's my back up husband. Maybe the shift in hormones is making me feel better too. I actually did some gardening this morning—nothing heavy, just trimming. I do get tired more easily but it felt good to be out there.

Stymied Again.
June 17, 2001
On my June 15 appointment I got really cruddy news. Couldn't even write about it until now. My ovaries weren't responding to the stimulation drugs so we had to pull the plug on the cycle. I feel such loss, pain anger. Yesterday I spent most of the day crying. I know this doesn't spell the end but I feel ended. Whenever I start my next cycle we'll try again with a different protocol—no suppression. I'm afraid to try again. Afraid of going through this again. So much body assault to lead to nothing. My stomach is still really bruised. I look like I went many rounds with Muhammed Ali in his prime. I know somewhere in here there must be some good but right now I'm pissed at the universe for all the heads up signs and now this. Thank the Goddess that my friend C was there when we got the news. She was stunned. I went numb right away, as if a large wave of "this can't be" was battling reality and it was too much. As she drove us home we held hands and cried. Crap. I'd much rather have been Thelma and Louise going off the cliff at that moment. There is still part of me that doesn't believe the news, and I find myself actually missing getting the shots because with the shots there is hope. Now hope for this cycle is ended and I feel tragedy.

Today I feel as if I got hit by a Mack truck and though I went for a long walk this morning my energy is about nil. I'm confused and angry and hurt and feel such loss, as if the undeveloped eggs died. Is the loss of potential any different than the loss of the actual? If I had to have loss this no doubt is better than having gone to the end and then having it not work.

For now, I'll let myself grieve and when I'm ready I'll look to trying again. This is a wild, difficult, ride.

in print format
http://www.amazon.com/-Vitro-Fertilization-Ultimate-Reality-uncensored/dp/1456419412

or on Kindle
http://www.amazon.com/Vitro-Fertlization-Ultimate-Reality-ebook/dp/B004LROPMC

Karen Daniels

From a Native American Prayer

We give you this one thought to keep—
We are with you still—we do not sleep.
We are a thousand winds that blow,
We are the diamond glints on snow,
We are the sunlight on ripened grain,
We are the gentle autumn rain.
When you awaken in the morning's hush,
We are the swift, uplifting rush
of quiet birds in circled flight.
We are the soft stars that shine at night.
Do not think of us as gone—We are with you still—
in each new dawn.

Printed in Great Britain
by Amazon.co.uk, Ltd.,
Marston Gate.